I truly loved reading Kay McSpadden's *Notes from a Classroom*. She is a special teacher who truly listens to her students, challenges them and makes them think. She teaches in this wonderful, creative way for all of her adolescent students—from Advanced Placement to Special Ed and all of those in between.

Every beginning or practicing teacher or student thinking about teaching would benefit from this book. As I read it, I had the same feelings as Kay's sixth grader who wrote on the poster in the classroom: "I love you, Teacher."

—Richard W. Riley
Former Governor of South Carolina
Former U.S. Secretary of Education

Kay McSpadden takes us inside a classroom, but even more, inside the mind of a classroom teacher who deals with the joys and tragedies of everyday life in rural South Carolina. Kay shows that the greatest teaching trait is love and respect. She loves her children and she respects and understands their shortcomings. Kay McSpadden is an example of a great teacher who gives hope to the next generation of children.

—Roy E. Barnes
Former Governor of Georgia
Founder, The Barnes Law Group, LLC

Remember the best qualities of the most influential teachers in your life, combine them and you have described Kay McSpadden, who loves her work, values her students, and writes about a teacher's life with passion, insight and delight. On rare occasions I read a book that leaves me feeling wiser. This is one of those books.

—Ed Williams
Editor of the Editorial Pages
The Charlotte Observer

The old adage of "words of wit and wisdom" truly applies to Kay McSpadden's reflections on her 30 years in the classroom. These are the thoughts and observations of a teacher who has thoroughly enjoyed her vocation as lion tamer of teenagers, wiper of tears, patter of backs, mother hen, counselor, applauder, corrector, motivator and demander of high standards.

(continued on next page)

Her love of knowledge, literature and her students comes through on every page. *Notes from a Classroom* is a joy for any teacher or student to read.

—Robert A. Preston
President Emeritus and Executive Director of the
Bradley Institute for the Study of Christian Culture at
Belmont Abbey College

In a time when teaching to tests is not only the norm but also the ideal, readers of *Notes from a Classroom* are fortunate to get to know a true teacher who is also a gifted writer. What comes through in all Kay McSpadden's essays are her wisdom, her understanding of human behavior, and her openness to learning—her own as well as her students'. Yet perhaps her greatest gift is showing us teachers and ordinary readers how literature reflects and enriches our lives.

—Joanne Yatvin
President
National Council of Teachers of English

Someone once said God was too busy to be everywhere so he invented grandmothers. As the human tribe spread across this earth nurses were invented to help heal us. But the best invention yet has got to be teachers. They are the angels who help make us civilized human beings. They are mother father sister brother nurse librarian friend and yes, bully. They make us learn but more they make us want to learn. What a treasure Kay McSpadden has given us. We laugh and cry and hope and understand with her all through her marvelous journey. Thank you, Kay, for your *Notes from a Classroom*. I'll hug a teacher today for you.

—Nikki Giovanni
Poet

Notes from a Classroom: Reflections on Teaching, Kay McSpadden's wonderful collection of stories of her (and her inspiring students) experiences in the classroom in rural South Carolina, should be required reading for all of us, whether we aspire to inspire as she has for 30 years in the classroom or simply want to remember why our best investment is in giving the future a chance to understand, discover and learn.

—Robert Hicks
New York Times Bestselling Author, *The Widow of the South*

Kay McSpadden has offered us a revealing view of high school teaching. All of us who are believers in secondary education can benefit from the revelations she has experienced in the classroom. Her thoughts are presented in a compelling and compassionate voice, one that can energize all of us who work or live with adolescents.

—Mel Levine, M.D.
Co-Chair and Co-Founder
All Kinds of Minds

Notes from a Classroom are not just notes but varied accounts of high school students and what it means to teach them. Mrs. McSpadden tells us she loves to talk, but she listens too and remembers.

—James V. Schall, S. J.
Professor of Government
Georgetown University

From these vignettes and analyses, we learn that Kay McSpadden is a learner herself who has cared enough to be a true teacher. We are fortunate that she has cared enough not only to teach our youth but also to compile her thoughts to attempt to teach us about the deepest joys of being a student.

— James W. Wagner
President
Emory University

For years I have been using Kay McSpadden's columns as examples and discussion-starters in my classes and posting them outside my office until they disintegrate. Thank you for making it possible to save and share these gems for many more years to come.

—Emily Seelbinder
Professor of English and 2007 winner of the Hunter-Hamilton
Love of Teaching Award at Queens University of Charlotte

Kay McSpadden's sparkling essays reveal her rare combination of mind and heart, intellect and compassion. Her genuine love of teaching and concern for her students will inspire anyone who cares what happens behind classroom doors—and that should be all of us.

— Jane McAlister Pope
Deputy Editor of the Editorial pages
The Charlotte Observer

For Randy, Jamie and Will

NOTES *from a* CLASSROOM

REFLECTIONS ON TEACHING

KAY MCSPADDEN

STAMPLEY

CHARLOTTE, NC

Most Stampley titles are available at special discounts when ordered in quantity for fundraising or educational use. Custom editions of this or other Stampley titles may also be commissioned for special occasions and needs.

For additional information, write:
Stampley, Special Markets, PO Box 33172, Charlotte, NC 28233
or email queries to sales@stampley.com.

Published by C.D. Stampley Enterprises, Inc., Charlotte, NC
www.stampley.com   /   info@stampley.com

www.notesfromaclassroom.com

Billy Collins, "Introduction to Poetry" from *The Apple That Astonished Paris*. Copyright © 1988, 1996 by Billy Collins. Used by permission of the University of Arkansas Press, www.uapress.com.

Cover design: Nils Lucander, Davidson, NC
Photograph of the author: Terry Roueche, Rock Hill, SC

Library of Congress Cataloging-in-Publication Data

McSpadden, Kay, 1956-
    Notes from a classroom : reflections on teaching / by Kay McSpadden.
        p. cm.
    Includes bibliographical references.
    ISBN 978-1-58087-131-0 (hardcover with dustjacket)
    1. Teaching. 2. Effective teaching. 3. English language--Study and teaching (Secondary) I. Title.

    LB1025.3.M397 2007
    371.102--dc22

2007028934

Printed in the United States of America

CONTENTS

Contents

Contents

Contents

ACKNOWLEDGMENTS

LIKE MOST OTHER EVENTS in our lives, publishing a book is an odyssey, a journey made possible with the guidance and help of numerous fellow travelers.

Many thanks to the editorial department of *The Charlotte Observer* and to Ed Williams, the Editorial Page Editor. Special thanks to Jane McAlister Pope, Deputy Editorial Page Editor, who gave me a chance to write for the paper and who continues to be my editor and friend. Thanks to the many readers of *The Charlotte Observer* who let me know when I hit or miss the mark.

Thanks to Scott Jagow and the listeners of WFAE who support local commentaries and National Public Radio.

This book is the brainchild of Rick Rotondi of Stampley, and would not have been possible without Crews Walden, Lydia Edsell, and Jose Morales. Many people read and commented on the manuscript, including Secretary Richard Riley, Governor Roy Barnes, Robert Preston, Joanne Yatvin, Nikki Giovanni, Robert Hicks, Mel

Levine, James Schall, S. J., Emily Seelbinder, and James Wagner, who also graciously granted permission to quote from his article which originally appeared in *The Atlanta Journal-Constitution*. Thanks to readers Christie Spivey, Peggy Reynolds, Sandy Rinck, Beth Donofrio, Betsy Rotondi, Linda Walden, and Laura Walden. Thanks also to Nils Lucander and Terry Roueche.

My family has been an unfailing source of encouragement: Randy, Jamie, and Will McSpadden; Charlie and Francis Darwin; Art Darwin; Tim Grana; and my sister Darlene Darwin, my childhood playmate and best fan.

Thanks to Marian Garner, who makes me a better teacher, and to my students, who remind me to never stop learning.

PREFACE

MY EARLIEST MEMORY is of being mute. Something had excited me and I was trying to tell my mother about it, but she smiled and ignored me. I tried again to tell her something and again she didn't understand what I was saying. My frustration was maddening.

I know enough about the mutability of memory to find this one suspect—but I have had it all my life, and whether or not it is genuine is unimportant. What is important is what the memory symbolizes about me—I have something to say.

I love to talk and apparently always have. My parents, whose memories of my talkativeness square with my own, told me often to stop talking so much and so loud. More than one of my elementary teachers wrote "Talks too much" on report cards.

Learning to listen has been a much harder skill than learning to talk. When I became a teacher, I inflicted far too much of myself on my students. Only gradually did I learn that they, too, had something to say. Once I started to listen, I started learning to teach.

I'm still learning.

I stepped into my first classroom in January 1977 as a long-term substitute for a class of emotionally handicapped sixth and seventh graders at a junior high in Lancaster, SC. The mental health issues that afflicted them were exacerbated by extreme poverty, and more than once I used my class time to take them to the high school cosmetology class to have their hair washed and trimmed and their fingernails cleaned and clipped.

My repertoire of teaching strategies for these children was almost nonexistent, so I spent my free time reading about disabilities and mental illness. No matter. The best plans often went awry, and I learned the value of improvising when my class threatened to disintegrate into chaos.

By May my students could at least sit through an entire class period without hitting someone—a skill we had practiced diligently—but they learned little else.

That fall I assumed another long-term substitute job, this time as a sixth grade language arts teacher. The kids were sweet—they argued every lunch period over who got to sit next to me—but I had the same maddening feeling that I had carried with me since I was a child—I was mute. I didn't know how to communicate with 11 and 12 year olds. I wanted to talk in abstractions; they thought in concrete terms. I wanted them to be independent and self-reliant; they often slipped up and called me Mama.

At the end of that year four English teachers left Chester High School in Chester, SC, and the principal was desperate. I met him and the personnel manager at the high school for a short interview.

"Can you wait out in the hall for a minute?" the principal asked, and almost as soon as I had stepped out of his office he called me back in to offer me a job.

At Chester High School I finally began to find my voice and hearing with teenagers. Although the children there suffered then—and suffer still—the effects of multigenerational poverty and neglect, I loved them. They were funny and streetwise, and they taught me how to laugh. They were short-sighted and foolish the way only teenagers can be, and they taught me to worry. They were stoic about the bleakness of their future, and I learned to cry for them. I left after three years only because my husband took a yearlong sabbatical to Nashville, TN, to earn a master's degree in social work.

When we returned to South Carolina, Chester High had no job openings, so I began working at York Comprehensive High. The only high school in York District #1, it is a high poverty school where over 60 percent of the students eat free or reduced-price lunch. The children in York aren't as impoverished as the children in Chester, but they are poor nevertheless. The effects of poverty in rural schools can be invisible but are still felt in the classroom. Children who have taken piano lessons, who have traveled or vacationed with their families, who have books and magazines at home, who have regular dental and health care, who have a parent to turn off the TV and send them to bed at a decent hour—those children excel in school. Children of poverty often don't, and they fall behind early and stay there. My students reveal their lives to me and their other teachers every time they walk into our classrooms, but many other people treat them as if they were as mute as I felt as a child.

Because their voices do matter, in the fall of 1998 I applied to be a community columnist in the *Charlotte Observer's* annual search for eight ordinary people to write monthly op-ed pieces for the Viewpoint page. We all went to school, I explained in my application, but only a few people know what goes on in schools today. I want to be that voice from the classroom, a voice of a teacher, but a voice for my students, too.

I want all the stakeholders in education, from parents to taxpayers, to know how their money is being spent. I want the public to see what is going right as well as what is going wrong in public education. I want other teachers to feel that they have a public voice as well, and while I am not a spokesman for anyone but myself, I believe that I do reflect the concerns that many teachers have.

And I want to do for readers what I try to do for my students; encourage them to look again at their assumptions, to examine their lives closely, to be as authentic as possible. I want to share with my readers the unique way that literature pricks us to think about the issues that we have in common: who are our heroes; what is justice; what separates love from hate; why do we choose to do good or evil; do we act freely or are our destinies fated; and who are we really?

Jane McAlister Pope, the deputy editor of the Viewpoint page, gave me a chance to be one of the eight columnists for the 1999 year, and she has generously allowed me to continue writing since then. This collection represents many of the different topics and stories that I shared with readers of the *Charlotte Observer*, as well as several radio commentaries recorded for WFAE, Charlotte's NPR affiliate. I hope they speak to you as well.

THE ART
OF
TEACHING

STUDENTS AS TEACHERS

January 7, 1999

MY STUDENTS KEEP ME HUMBLE. When I told my classes that I had been selected to write a monthly column for the *Charlotte Observer*, not a single student seemed as impressed as I was with myself. Perhaps they wanted to spare me the humiliation of falling off a pedestal by not elevating me there to begin with. In their good hearted teenager way, they remind me daily that if we really do learn from our mistakes, then I will always be the smartest person in my high school classroom.

As well as my current students, the ghosts and memories of students past keep chipping away at my narcissism. Some of the most poignant memories come from my first teaching job, which began in January 1977 after the teacher for the emotionally handicapped class at a Lancaster County junior high abruptly left and refused to return. That should have been a clue to me, but I was a

December graduate with bills and rent due, so I took the job out of my field of English education and received a one year temporary teaching certificate in special education. I cried every day on the way to work, and I cried even harder on the way home. I learned quickly that all my education and idealism were worthless in a classroom with children so damaged. I shudder to remember how little I taught those students—certainly they learned no reading skills or math facts from me that semester. At night I crammed every special education book I could find: The next day I used my class as human guinea pigs and tried one behavior modification technique after another. To her credit, my aide, a skeptical woman twice my age and much wiser in many things, went along with my charts and rewards, my learning centers and timeout areas, and after several months we did manage to eliminate the overt violence that these students tried to inflict on each other and themselves. A considerable portion of my salary that year went to buy cookies, pens, candy, stickers—whatever motivated the class to sit for an hour and attempt to read or reason with minds so bashed by the emotional storms that would haunt them long after they left junior high. Only a few months ago one of them made headlines as a murder victim, killed by a relative who was alarmed by his increasingly bizarre behavior. My inability to offer a more hopeful future for those students has left me with a dark conviction that education cannot cure poverty or disease, abuse or neglect. Our limitations as educators are galling.

That first year was followed by another year out of my field, this time teaching sixth grade language arts students. I'm sure I must have done some things right that year, but all I can remember is something I did very wrong. One day as my students were coming into the room during a class change, I noticed a little girl writing on a poster on my wall. As soon as the bell rang and the class settled down, I scolded the student as harshly as I could. I yammered on and on about the destruction of personal property, personal responsibility, my own personal disappointment with her. When I was satisfied that the student seemed teary and contrite enough, I walked to the poster and read her graffiti: "I love you, Teacher." That memory, which still causes me deep pain, has served me well over the years. When I am tempted to snap at my students or hold them accountable for things beyond their control, I remember those early years of patience learned the hard way.

Being patient with teenagers isn't easy. Teenagers can be the worst people in the world—contrary, obnoxious, horrifyingly honest. My students don't hesitate to comment on my physical appearance ("Did you get a new haircut, Mrs. McSpadden? It looks really weird") or my teaching abilities ("Why did you make us read this dumb story?"). A friend told me recently that the best advice I ever gave her when she started teaching was to remind herself every day that a teenager's job is to be difficult and rebellious at times. Their moodiness and attitudes are partly a necessary developmental stage in the uncomfortable journey to independence. Remembering my own miserable teenage years helps me deal with my students in their distressing moments, and I assure them that any adults who tell them "these are the best years of your life" are either forgetful or dishonest.

Yet teenagers are the best people, too. Too often adults have hardened their opinions into dogma; teenagers are more willing to consider the troubling issues of truth and justice, good and evil, fate and free will—all universal concerns which make discussions in an English classroom dynamic and liberating. Though they might posture and pretend their confidence, most young people know at some level that they have things to ponder and learn before leaving the sanctuary of high school. That openness is what makes working with them such a pleasure—the joy when a student says, "That poem says exactly what I feel"; the delight of inspiring an entire class to sit together at lunch to continue a debate cut short by the bell.

More than any college education class, more than any new research on learning styles, more than any workshops on classroom management, my students have taught me how to teach. Even the unsuccessful classes are instructive, if not to my students, then at least to me. Just as teaching has offered me many lessons in humility, I have a strong feeling that writing this monthly column will be the same roller coaster of successes and failures. If it is anything like teaching, it ought to be a fun ride.

GREAT EXPECTATIONS

August 5, 1999

TODAY CHARLOTTE-MECKLENBURG teachers add their cars to the morning traffic and report to the world of the employed. Teachers in neighboring school districts also start a new school year this week or will soon, and students pack their bookbags and join them shortly. Gone are the days when the Back to School sale signs were a comfortable lie when they appeared by July 4th. Gone are the days when Labor Day was the last kiss of summer vacation.

Among those teachers gearing up for a new year are a special group of people, many of them born the year I started teaching. These young people are not yet teachers, though they have diplomas which indicate their mastery of special curricula and the certificates required by the state examiners. This morning as they meet their fellow faculty members and sit in meetings or put up posters on their very own classroom walls, they may at times feel like impostors. They worry about living on a teacher's salary, making friends in a new city, staying alive the first day that those now-empty classrooms teem with squirmy kids. They try to peer into the future to see what they should do, how they can become real teachers—not just in name only.

I have never been very good at looking into the future, but my hindsight is 20/20. I can see with startling clarity every misstep, every wrong turn, every bad decision in my past. My mistakes have become channel markers and constellations to help me navigate my own teaching career. Surely my gifted backwards clairvoyance can benefit any novice teachers who may feel at sea.

To those young people embarking on a life of teaching, my advice culled from 22 years of successes and failures is simple: Keep your expectations high, for yourself as a teacher, for your school, and most of all, for your students.

Students rise or fall to the level of our expectations for them, too. Teachers who expect their students to be successful engineer that success with ample opportunities for active engagement in the lesson. They set up classrooms which require participation and then refuse to be the only participant. New teachers, especially, are tempted to demonstrate their own mastery of the material in talking-head performances and are disappointed by the glazed looks they get from unappreciative, bored students. Instead, having high expectations for students means giving them as much responsibility for the learning as they can handle—dividing up the lesson and letting them present their findings to their peers, or encouraging students to explore a particular problem without rushing in to solve it for them.

Finally, to all the new teachers, expect this year to be quite a journey. Whether you expect it or not, your students will teach you how to teach. Children are not masters of the subtle—they will tell you in word and misdeed when you are failing; you will know you are succeeding when they tolerate your jokes or humor your experimental lesson plans. They will be your harshest critics and your staunchest defenders. Once you have their loyalty, you will have allies who will work to meet your expectations and will feel remorse when they let you down.

When you have that kind of relationship with your students, you will be a teacher.

THE FIRST YEAR

June 4, 2005

YESTERDAY WHEN YORK'S CLASS OF 2005 marched across the stage to receive their diplomas, their teachers smiled proudly at them and gave a collective sigh of relief and sorrow. It's the same every year, this mix of feelings as we watch our students walk out of our lives and into their future.

This year's graduation was an important milestone for one of the teachers watching those exiting seniors. Lauren Klepinger survived her first year of teaching high school English.

In addition to the stress of being a newlywed with a mortgage payment, she survived the flu, strep throat, and so many respiratory infections that she lost count. She never got enough sleep. Studying and grading papers took all of her free time. Managing a classroom of teenagers took all of her energy. A daily lunch regimen of institution chicken nuggets took its toll.

And yet, when I sat down with Lauren this week to ask about her year, she was upbeat, reflective, ready to recuperate over the summer and return recharged in August.

"I will do so many things differently," she said. "I've learned so much this year."

Her biggest surprise has been the staggering workload. Lauren taught British and American literature, two subjects she already knows well, but knowing how to teach them to sometimes indifferent teenagers is another matter. She often fell asleep with a textbook in the bed, and when she wasn't reading, she was planning lessons—setting objectives, typing up worksheets, designing group activities, writing discussion questions.

Sometimes all her planning was greeted with yawns or bafflement, but more often than not her students responded positively to her youth and energy, and by the end of the year, she was feeling more and more successful.

She was also more successful in simply dealing with teenagers as the year went on, more sure-footed navigating the tightrope between firmness and fairness. Once or twice she felt herself on the brink of tears with a particularly challenging student, but she never lost control, never lost sight of herself as the head of her classroom.

I've known Lauren for many years, since she was a sophomore in my American literature class, and she brings to her teaching the same qualities that made her an outstanding student—intelligence, courage, and above all, a willingness to learn. If at first she felt awkward working side-by-side with her own teachers, she was quickly accepted as a fellow faculty member, joining several of my brightest former students who are now my colleagues. In fact, our faculty is especially collegial and our administration is very supportive, a happy situation for any teacher, but a necessary one if a new teacher is going to thrive.

The English department has spent many lunches listening sympathetically as Lauren has shared with us her frustrations, and, always eager to talk, we have given her far more advice than she probably wanted. Lauren's willingness to ask for help—and her frank acceptance of her own need to learn and grow in her profession—make me confident that she will not become a statistic, one of the 60 percent of new teachers who leave education within three years.

Lauren went into teaching with a clearer view of the frustrations and rewards than most people ever see. Her mother, Susan Huntley, is a popular seventh grade language arts teacher, and her father, Dan, writes for the *Charlotte Observer*. Both careers called when Lauren was in college—she majored in English and journalism—but teaching tugged her harder.

"I know I'm where I'm supposed to be," she said.

Her students would agree. Recently one of them gave her a beautiful drawing with a note explaining that Lauren's English class was the first one she had ever enjoyed. This student—a senior—had gone all through school without appreciating a poem, without reading a novel for pleasure, without writing an essay with conviction, but Lauren's energy and enthusiasm touched her in a way none of the rest of us had.

This, more than anything else, is why I'm grateful that Lauren is part of my department. Sure, beginning teachers may not be as graceful or as organized as experienced teachers, but their zeal and passion are powerful models for everyone tempted to slip into complacency. They may have a great deal to learn, but they also have plenty to teach the rest of us about the dangers of letting our content become shopworn, or assuming that we don't need to approach every lesson, every student, with a belief in possibility.

THE AMEN CORNER

March 4, 1999

WHEN I WAS A CHILD, I drank enough of the Atlantic Ocean trying to body surf that I should have become an expert on judging waves. A tentative, inept swimmer, I managed to pickle my insides with salt water gulped during regular wipeouts. Often I spent an afternoon scraping my knees raw chasing a receding tide whose waves were too spent to push me to shore.

But what kept me going back into the surf was the hope that the tide would turn and begin to surge in, pushing tons of turbocharged waves and me forward in a speedy race to the beach. Those few minutes when the low tide began its turn were eerie—large green rolls of water bobbing by without curling. Then the sea would seem to make a decision to return to the shore in waves so forceful that they could pin me under if I didn't jump into them at just the right moment. It was exhilarating and terrifying.

The same thing is true for teaching.

With each new classroom, teachers face an unknown ocean, sure only of its beauty and fearsome power. Drowning seems a very real possibility.

This year, I sank like a rock the first time I met with my fourth period class. My students were wary, ready to retreat, hesitant about participating or becoming involved. They pulled away as quickly as any receding tide ever had. "Make us care," they seemed to say. I began by asking them to write a letter about themselves. "Tell me who you are, what you like, what you don't like," I said. They reluctantly pulled out paper and sighed.

"Dear Mrs. McSpadden," Josh wrote, "I am interested in many things, and English isn't one of them."

Since then, I have been treading water, my headway toward the shore small but perceptible as those students and I have become comfortable with each other. We've established that I'm the lead dog; the class clowns have learned to contain their outbursts, at least more often than not; everyone knows the class rules and routines and reminds me when I stray from them. Most importantly, we've also had those defining moments when I know I am gathering allies to my side and the rest of the class will soon follow.

I was aware of the shifting tide the day I asked a student to stop chatting and he did, for a minute. When he began again, Josh turned to him and scolded, "She done told you to hush." The talker hushed; the rest of the class nodded their approval. He didn't speak standard English, perhaps, but Josh communicated quite effectively. "I'll give you a chance," he was telling me.

From that day on, that class has had what I like to think of as the Amen Corner. These are the majority of students who really do want to learn, who brook no foolishness from potential goof-offs. Their endorsement of the teacher and the class is like the gathering force of the incoming tide, and a lucky teacher recognizes this and takes advantage of it.

"Now, you know that many of you are seniors sitting here in junior English because you failed last year," I begin, and the Amen Corner shake their heads ruefully with remorse for their past misdeeds.

"That doesn't mean," I continue, "that you have to fail again."

"That's right," one Amen Cornerer nods in agreement. "I ain't never did this good in English before."

His comment catches me off-guard, but in this context, content wins over form. I go on.

"Tomorrow you will have an in-class essay test on these contemporary poets we have been reading. Study the notes you took, look over your worksheets, and you will ace this test."

"I can do this!" a senior member states enthusiastically.

"I didn't take any notes," one unsaved soul mumbles sheepishly. "I lost all the worksheets."

Before I can respond, the Amen Corner turns on the unfortunate sinner and lights into him. They are beyond trying to convert him; they simply want him to understand his damnation. "Why didn't you take notes?" they demand. "Where's your notebook? Why do you put your head down and try to sleep? She can't do the work for you!"

Suddenly I am ten years old again, and the best wave of the afternoon has just swelled under my arms and propelled me forward with dizzying momentum. This is the communion that teachers long for, sea to swimmer, mind to mind; all the water-choked near-drownings remote and unimportant now as the beach looms only a toehold away.

Amen.

PERKS

September 10, 2005

SOME YEARS BACK my former brother-in-law worked as a phone techie for a software giant in Charlotte. All day long he sat in a cubicle and tried to diagnose and solve computer problems for unhappy customers. Like too many computer geeks that I know, he was impatient with his clients, often belittling their intelligence and dismissing their concerns. He complained bitterly that his own considerable powers were being wasted on helping stupid people sort through obvious messes, and he longed for the day when his supervisors would promote him out of the techie pool into a better job doing something real, such as designing software.

When he wasn't complaining about the actual work, my brother-in-law liked to praise the perks that made the job bearable.

"They give us all the free Diet Coke we want," he told

me often, and though he claimed that the company cool-
er also stocked free beer on Fridays, I was skeptical. The
company dining hall served gourmet food cooked by well-
known chefs. The health insurance was fabulous, and
each year employees were awarded shares of stock as part
of their benefits package. My brother-in-law spent his
days in a beautiful office with soft music and warm lights
and comfortable furniture.

When he talked too long about the joys of his job, I
always tried to steer him back to its miseries.

"What about that woman who called and swore her
computer didn't have an On button?" I might say. "Remember how she screamed at you? Or that guy who was sure his
mouse was broken, but it wasn't even plugged in. Remember him?"

And then I could sit back with satisfaction and watch
my brother-in-law's face fall.

"I hate that job," he would say, and I would sigh happily. Free beer, indeed. No one deserves soft music at
work, much less unlimited soft drinks.

If that seems an uncharitable attitude, remember that
I have spent my adult life working for public school systems, places not known for their perks. So far this year has
been no exception.

The teachers in my district returned to school the
second week of August, but in my high school, the carpets
that had been cleaned in June were still wet. The air was
so heavy with water vapor that the posters had peeled off
the walls. Mold and mildew had ruined books and maps.

I bought a dehumidifier for my classroom and dumped out two gallons of water a day.

By the time the students arrived a week later, the carpets were merely damp and much of the mildew had been wiped up. The air conditioner in my windowless, fluorescent-lit classroom made the air chilly and uncomfortable, but at least it wasn't like the hallway, hot and steamy.

"We don't need bells and whistles," a voter wrote to the local paper two years ago, explaining why he helped defeat a bond referendum that would have replaced this ailing, overcrowded building.

I think of his comment often.

I thought of his comment when I looked over my rolls before school started and was alarmed that I had 31 students listed for my Applied Communications III class, a course for poorly performing juniors. Ideally such a class should be smaller than usual, allowing the teacher more time to assess and interact with students individually. Instead, this particular class was designated an inclusion class, meaning that a special education teacher had been assigned to team-teach it with me.

If you were designing a class to be the setting for some sort of devious teacher survivor show, you would create a class exactly like this one. It meets third period and is assigned second lunch, which means that the students have already sat through two 90-minute classes before they come to me to sit through another 90-minute class before eating lunch at 1:30. Half of the class are special education students with serious learning disabilities that keep them from reading or writing well. The other half are resentful seniors who failed English last year. When student number 32 walked in the second day of school, the special education teacher had to give up her desk and book to him—though we rarely sit in this class, needing, instead, to circle the room constantly like two sharks, keeping everyone on task.

Yet three weeks into school, the students are so delightful that I don't think about the missing perks of the job. When I say that the students are delightful, I don't mean that they are all pleasant or polite, or that they love school. I mean that they have all bought into the program, that everyone works at whatever assignment I set before them, that they believe me when I tell them that this is the year they will be successful.

For now, at least, they share my vision of the future, one where even the most challenged student improves his skills, where the least engaged student finds a lesson that piques his interest. As long as they do—no matter how cramped or uncomfortable the classroom, no matter how far away lunchtime seems—I'm happy to be there with them.

EUREKA STORIES

March 29, 2001

PICTURE THIS. A bathtub filled to the brim with steamy water. A tired mathematician, stepping in and easing himself down slowly. A waterfall cascades over the sides, and Archimedes, with original insight into the principle of displacement, yells, "Eureka!" Later, after his bath, he scribbles some notes foreshadowing Newton and calculus, and modern life as we know it is practically fated.

As a teacher, I am a sucker for these eureka stories, true or not, descriptions of storms of confusion and frustration illuminated by lightning flashes of clarity. Ask any teacher to describe the greatest pleasure in a classroom and you will hear about the joy of watching students when their faces light up with genuine realizations. Every teacher has a repertoire of accounts of dreary lessons transformed into celebrations of teaching and learning when the students looked up in sudden wonder and said, "I get it now!"

What I have sometimes forgotten to catalog are my own eureka moments, my struggles to learn the best way to teach. As much as I may wish to present my evolution as a teacher as the result of hours of reading professional journals and systematic academic study, I have to admit that much of what I know about students and about myself as a teacher has been the result of serendipity— goofy mistakes that somehow ended up working better than expected, or accidents that landed my way and demanded action.

And those moments continue to happen.

Recently, for example, my technological incompetence helped me discover a nifty teaching tool. I wanted to show the movie version of *Sense and Sensibility* to my English IV class as a bridge between our study of 18th century British literature, a time of great "sense" and scientific inquiry, and the early 19th century Romantic poets who valued "sensibility" and intuition.

For some reason, the television was set to show closed captions the day we began the movie, and despite my best efforts, I couldn't turn them off. I found them maddening, but my students seemed unusually involved in the plot of the movie. They were amused, indignant, and outraged at all the right places—and no one tried to sleep. Since the extra work of decoding the words appeared to help my students comprehend the plot, I resolved to put aside my own annoyance and continue to use the closed captions.

The next day, of course, nothing I nor my more tech-savvy students could do could get the closed captions back

on, and the mood in the classroom was noticeably damp-
ened. The students lost the simple threads of conversations.
They were baffled by the characters' predicaments, and
worse, they were indifferent. By the end of class, several
heads were bobbing.

On the last day of the movie, I made sure that the
librarian set the television before class began, and the students were as lively as they had been the first day, proudly predicting the complications and resolutions in the
story. Their obvious enjoyment of the intricacies of Jane
Austen's novel was one of those rare, almost sacramental
moments of communion.

Now, I am no Archimedes. I have stepped into the tub
and seen the water gush over the sides, and I know that
the two actions are connected. Every time I want to push
water out of the tub, I know how to do it. But I can't go
on to create calculus. I can't create some overarching theory of literacy or human brain function on the basis of
observations of what has worked or failed in my classroom. What I can do, however, is have the librarian teach
me how to cue the closed captions so that I can use them
the next time I show a movie to my students.

While I welcome the newest research on how we
learn and I applaud the science that drives it, my own
experiences in the classroom make me skeptical of quick-
fix solutions and fads which promise easy cures for education's woes.

In a recent series on literacy, for example, National
Public Radio aired reports on two low-performing schools

on opposite sides of the country which recently had made unexplained gains on standardized test scores, even though each had adopted radically different approaches to teaching reading.

One school immersed the first graders in long stretches of undirected reading and then culled from the students themselves the stories they wanted to study. The goal was to promote reading for pleasure as a starting point for teaching critical thinking skills.

Another school had a tightly structured curriculum with interwoven vocabulary drills and scripted lessons for the teachers to follow. The emphasis was on phonics and grammar.

All of the students flourished. Opposite strategies, similar results. No eureka, no definite explanation. Perhaps, the experts speculate, the passion the teachers bring to the classroom is what matters more than any theory or curriculum or gimmick.

And the hallmark of that passion? The belief that no one, not even the teacher, should ever stop learning something new.

ALLIES

November 1, 2003

SOMEWHERE IN THE BOTTOM of a drawer in my desk at school is a student essay written so long ago that it is stiff and yellow with age. I've kept it as a reminder that parents are necessary partners in their children's education—and as a testament to the power of a single conversation.

The author of the essay, Tim, was a brilliant student in my Advanced Placement English class, and like some other brilliant students I have taught over the years, he had become lazy and indifferent in school, able to match the grades of his less capable peers with little effort. He was charming and witty, such as the time I overheard him offering his explanation on why the 50-year-old French teacher looked so young.

"The woman must drink Oil of Olay," he quipped.

The year had barely started when I assigned Tim's class their first major essay. While the other students met with me before and after school for conferences to check their outlines and drafts, Tim cobbled together his paper in a few minutes during homeroom the day it was due. When I handed it back the next day, Tim was not only shocked, he was outraged. I had actually written more on his paper than he had—long notes and examples in red ink—but the grade was what offended him.

"How could my essay get an F?" he asked angrily. I offered to go through it point by point with him but Tim was too mad.

That evening Tim's father called me, as furious as Tim had been. I couldn't get a word in for several minutes while he ranted and raved about public education in general and about me in particular. Finally he stopped for a breath and I jumped in.

"Tim is far too smart to turn in junk like this," I said. "That F is a measure of the distance between what he did and what he can do. You would be disappointed in me as his teacher if I accepted anything less than his best."

Tim's father was so quiet that for a moment I thought he had hung up. Then a miracle happened.

"You're right," his father said, and for the next ten minutes I couldn't get a word in as he apologized and promised that from now on we would be allies in Tim's education.

And we were. When I made Tim revise his essay— and it took him 13 revisions to get it nearly perfect—his father told him to stop whining and get busy.

I think about Tim and his father every time my school has an Open House or a Parent Conference Day and only a few people show up. Although research suggests a strong correlation between parental involvement and student success, many parents stay away for a variety of reasons. Some are too busy with work or family commitments; others feel intimidated by schools and teachers, especially if their own educational experience was unhappy.

Even those parents who regularly visit their children's elementary schools sometimes drop away when their kids enter high school, mistakenly thinking that their older children don't need or want as much attention.

One mother with a son in high school was so reluctant to check on his progress in his difficult college preparatory classes this year that she let half of the first grading period slip away before she contacted his teachers. She worried that the teachers would be annoyed with her e-mails or would find her questions intrusive.

That mother was me. I understand the reluctance parents may feel about seeking out their children's teachers, even though—ironically—as a teacher I have always welcomed that same sort of parental contact and involvement.

When I finally talked to my son's teachers and expressed my concerns, they were gracious and helpful. More important than what I said to them, the message I gave my son was that his success in school means demanding nothing less than the best, from him and from me.

If you have children in school, you want them to hear that same message. Make it clear by attending Parents' Night and e-mailing or calling your children's teachers whenever you have a question or a comment. Know when report cards are issued—most schools have websites or newsletters to keep you posted. Look at your children's homework without doing it for them and ask them what they are learning in school.

Encourage your children to take the most challenging classes available, and if they need extra help to succeed, don't be shy about asking the schools for it.

As for Tim, I found out recently that after he graduated from college he went on to teach high school English.

If, indeed, converted sinners are the most zealous of all, woe be to any of his students whose aim is low and lazy!

TEACHABLE MOMENTS

April 23, 2005

THEY CALL THEMSELVES REDNECKS. I prefer the term "good ole boys." Either way, they revel in being stereotypical, in offering a visual shorthand of the quintessential rural kid.

They are the boys in my senior English class.

Their hair is short, and if the school would let them, they would smash it under their John Deere caps all day. They wear jeans or overalls and boots, belts with buckles as big as saucers, tee shirts that advertise farm equipment or race car heroes.

They spend part of their day in high school refining skills they already have—planting crops and raising cattle, tuning up cars and building cabinets. For many of them, English is the only academic class they take this last semester before graduation.

But there the stereotype stops. These boys, so talented with their hands and so restless in a regular classroom, have excelled in English literature, can turn out a short but grammatical essay during a timed test, and read voraciously. In fact, the biggest discipline problem I have with them is that after the first fifteen minutes of class—our sustained silent reading time—they hide their novels behind their textbooks to continue reading.

The other day one of these boys told me as he came in the door that the book he was reading was the best he had ever read in his life.

"You mean it is the only book you've ever read," I teased, and he quickly protested.

"Oh, no, I've read more books this year than I ever have."

He went on to tell me that the book was *The Land* by Mildred Taylor, and I mentioned that he might also enjoy her other novels, *Roll of Thunder, Hear My Cry*, and *Let the Circle Be Unbroken*.

"I don't know," he said. "My reading spell is almost over."

I knew immediately what he meant. This bright boy, this interested reader, did not imagine a future where he would read for pleasure. His world would be busy, physical, strenuous, enjoyable—but reading a novel was something he did in English class when the teacher insisted that he do it and gave him the time when he must. My heart sank a little, knowing that reading for enjoyment might not be an activity he would carry with him to adulthood.

A few days later I felt like a failure again with this class, this time because I missed what in educationese is

called "the teachable moment." The class was studying
Alfred Tennyson, a poet who often embraces the conven-
tional morality and religious attitudes of the Victorians
but who also reveals frank uncertainty about those same
ideas. We had read *Ulysses*, which ends with what could
be called the Victorian mantra—"to strive, to seek, to find,
and not to yield"—and were wrestling with Tennyson's
more troubling poems in the collection *In Memoriam*.
These poems deal with the sudden, devastating loss of his
best friend, Arthur Henry Hallam, when both were very
young men. How could the same person who wrote such
defiant words in *Ulysses* also call himself an "infant crying
in the night"?

"I don't understand that," one of my good ole boys
said. "I don't even comprehend it."

His friends howled.

"That's the same thing!" they said, but he was
adamant. You could almost hear the banjos when they
whipped out their dictionaries from under their desks and
began dueling.

"Look here," the Mildred Taylor fan pointed, "the definition of comprehend has the word understand in it."

"I don't care," the good ole boy retorted.
"Comprehend is bigger!"

And that's where I missed my chance. These boys
were wrestling with the kind of critical thinking they will
need for the rest of their lives. They knew that words have
subtleties, but they couldn't articulate exactly what they
wanted to say. I thought briefly about reminding them of

the terms "denotation" and "connotation." They had even memorized a mnemonic device to help them distinguish between the two—denotation starts with a D because it means the dictionary meaning. Connotations are the fuzzy edges, the shades of meaning, the flavors and feelings evoked by words. How many times had they heard these terms explained over the years? How many times had they understood them but not comprehended them?

I could have stopped and nailed that point home, made those two concepts finally mean something tangible in their everyday lives, in their heated argument with each other. I could have given them another layer of complexity when they tried to speak their minds, handed them a tool to use in evaluating what they hear and read as adults, but instead I laughed for a minute and then shushed them up. The curriculum train was blowing its whistle, the wheels starting to turn, and we were getting left at the station.

"We have a test Tuesday," I said primly, hurrying them off the platform and back into the train car, "and we have lots to cover before then."

GRADING

May 21, 2005

IT'S A LOSE-LOSE SITUATION that didn't have to happen. The board of education in Gwinnett County, Georgia, spent part of Teacher Appreciation Week debating what to do about Larry Neace.

Neace, a physics teacher for the past 23 years at Dacula High School, instructed his students to complete an assignment during the last twenty minutes of class. Two students went to sleep instead. As the bell was about to ring, Neace told his students that they could use the first ten minutes of class the next day to finish. When the two sleeping students turned in perfect assignments, Neace lowered their grade by half. The father of one of the students complained and the principal called Neace into a conference.

The principal argued that school and district policy forbids using grades as punishment, and sleeping in class is a discipline problem, not an academic matter.

Neace argued that school and district policy allows teachers to give class participation grades. The sleeping students were not participating in the corporate life of the class and were marked accordingly. His students sign a syllabus which explains his policy of factoring in "wasting time or sleeping" as part of their grades. For at least ten years he has maintained this policy without any complaints from administrators or parents.

The principal then told Neace that even so, he had to change the student's grade.

Neace refused. Changing a grade for any reason other than a computational error is grounds for losing a teaching license in many counties, he argued.

At that point Larry Neace was told to leave his school and to wait for his hearing before the school board.

On May 6, he was fired for insubordination.

"What this case really boils down to is, who is the boss," Vicki Sweeny, attorney for the school district said later.

Neace's lawyers suggest a more sinister motive.

"What we have in this case is a case of a pampered football athlete sleeping in class and being given favored treatment on an academic grade. What we have here is the principal essentially attempting to coerce and intimidate a teacher," said Michael M. Kramer, one of Neace's lawyers.

Many observers agree that this case highlights some of the tricky problems that teachers navigate in the classroom. Do certain groups of students get special treatment? Do parents and administrators sometimes pressure teachers to alter grades? Could both sides in the Larry Neace case have found common cause in a less confrontational setting?

Yes, yes, and yes. What is not so clear is the stickier issue of how grades and behavior are connected in the first place.

Most teachers would agree with attorney Sweeny when she said that "if a teacher deducts points from the grade because of a student's conduct, you do not get an accurate portrayal of a student's achievement." But teachers also recognize that the truly accurate grade, the one which is an authentic, objective measure of a student's performance, is the Holy Grail in education, and probably just as elusive.

Grades are affected all the time by student behavior. A student leaves out questions on a test because he doesn't have time to finish. Does that test accurately measure what he knows, or does it show how fast he can work? A student loses points for turning in a major project late, or gets a zero on homework left sitting on his desk at home. Are those grades genuine measures of his academic achievement? A student has a streaming head cold, or he is worried about the argument that he overheard his parents having that morning, or he woke up late and didn't have time to eat anything before school. Everything that student does that day to demonstrate his academic achievement—every test he takes, every essay he writes, every answer he gives in every class—is influenced by his behavior as he wrestles with his real life, and pretending otherwise is ridiculous.

Students are also aware that their behavior can influence their grades in a positive way. Occasionally students ask me to grade them on effort, for example. I realize that their request is an indication of their frustration with the assignment and their inability to be as successful in the outcome as they would like. However, I refuse those requests—after all, I tell my students, I don't have an Effort-o-Meter that would help me sort out the more diligent students from the gifted fakers.

In the case of Larry Neace, Gwinnett County needs to decide if allowing for a participation grade is a benefit or a hindrance to authentic assessment. They've already lost a talented teacher over that slippery slope.

And all of us in education would do well to have a real discussion about how we can more accurately assess student achievement, recognizing that our touted objectivity is too often more myth than reality.

PLAGIARISM

March 16, 2002

MANY YEARS AGO when I was more naive in the classroom than I am now, I was shocked when a junior English student turned in a paper which included this sentence: *Volcanoes are formed when molten rock escapes (see next page) to the surface of the earth through cracks in the crust.* The sentence was not in quotation marks, nor was it footnoted in any way.

Initially I was very angry, but the plagiarism was so stupid and obvious that I pulled the student aside to talk. He seemed surprised and said, "What's the matter? That's what it said in the *World Book*. I've always written reports from encyclopedias."

I learned several valuable lessons that day.

I learned that students could read without comprehending. "See next page" in the middle of the text was proof of that.

I learned that students could steal without recognizing their guilt. My student didn't hesitate to own up to his debt to the encyclopedia because he saw nothing wrong with what he had done.

Finally, I learned that I was partly to blame for what had happened. I had spent a class session talking to my students about plagiarism and showing them examples before we ever began researching their topics, assuming—wrongly—that showing a teenager something one time was sufficient.

Since then I've changed the way I assign research projects, grading the process as well as the final product. Now I require that my students turn in their notecards periodically before they create an outline or a rough draft, making plagiarism easier to catch, particularly the unintentional kind when students adopt the unique phrases of a writer and forget to document the actual words correctly. Likewise, I read every rough draft and check for appropriate documentation. By the time I get the final papers, I have no surprises.

That approach might have spared a Kansas teacher from a classroom debacle that has ended in her resignation from teaching altogether. Christine Pelton, a second year teacher at Piper High School, noticed similarities in the papers turned in by 28 of her 118 biology students. She submitted the papers to an Internet data base which is designed to identify plagiarism and her suspicions were confirmed.

Pelton gave zeros to the biology projects which included plagiarized papers, and because the projects counted half of the semester grade, those students failed the course.

Although both the principal and the school superintendent supported the teacher's decision, the school board intervened when parents complained and directed Pelton to give zeros only to the papers themselves instead of the entire biology projects. Furthermore, they told her to recalculate the weight of the projects from 50 to 30 percent of the semester average.

While the school board's directions are not in themselves bad ideas—even Pelton's advocates have questioned the wisdom of having a single project weighted this heavily—their timing so seriously undermined her authority that she resigned immediately, saying that she felt unsupported while following the district's policy for cheating.

On the other hand, the parents who went to the school board claimed that their children weren't cheating. Theresa Woolley, who described her daughter as an A student, said that paraphrasing and documenting cited work is confusing for students. Certainly some students plagiarize because of laziness or even bravado, but because of my own experiences with my students, I don't dismiss Woolley's comments out of hand. In fact, when Pelton confronted some of her students about vocabulary that seemed uncharacteristic for them in their papers, they admitted both that they didn't know what the phrases meant and that they had taken them from Internet sites, sounding more confused than sneaky.

In retrospect, the school board could have validated

the teacher while addressing the concerns of the parents by having the students redo the project papers and saving the changes in how the projects are weighted for next year—particularly since changing that rule after students had completed the projects seems unfair to those who did well.

Some will argue that allowing the students to redo their papers is too lenient and sends a message that cheating is acceptable. They may be right, though making the slackers do the work they tried to avoid and letting the misguided have another chance is appealing.

Certainly students are not the only ones plagiarizing these days, as the recent Stephen Ambrose and Doris Kearns Goodwin instances show. Neither of those highly-regarded historians can claim that they misunderstood the definition of plagiarism, yet both have had to publicly apologize to other authors whose material they passed off as their own.

Even issues of digital piracy and the theft of intellectual property revisit the same territory as plagiarism—when do the creator's rights for credit and compensation outweigh the public's need for access to information? Legislation, such as the newest ban on unlimited digital copying sponsored by Democratic Senator Fritz Hollings, or Internet data base sites which scan submitted papers to identify plagiarized material, will not be able to stymie every determined thief. The best we might be able to do for now is to educate the accidental thieves in our classrooms and watch over their shoulders a little more carefully as they learn to value the written word.

THEN YOU'LL DIE EDUCATED

July 3, 2004

I SAW HER out of the corner of my eye, a tall woman hesitantly waving while I stood in the checkout line at the grocery store.

"Mrs. McSpadden?" she said, and when I turned to look at her, I recognized her as a student from many years ago.

"You'll have to tell me your name," I said sheepishly, but she did not seem to mind.

She told me that since high school she has been busy with a job in Charlotte and with raising three sons. While we talked her eyes flicked away briefly as if she were looking for something, and suddenly her face lit up and she motioned to a man pushing a buggy to join us.

"This is my husband," she said, and he smiled shyly.

"I had to meet you," he told me, "because she said you were one of the sweet teachers at school."

For a moment I thought I must have misheard him, but she added, "Yeah, you were so sweet to me."

I am not a sweet teacher. Very few of my students—except those whose memories have been softened by age—would say that I am.

Some of my most shameful moments as a teacher have been missed opportunities to speak to a student in pain, to acknowledge someone's distress. Too often I have been a blind teacher.

I would like to be a sweet teacher, someone like Harry Potter's favorite professor, Remus Lupin, the Defense Against the Dark Arts teacher whose lessons are both practical and interesting. When Lupin first shows up in *Harry Potter and the Prisoner of Azkaban*, the students at Hogwarts Academy for Witchcraft and Wizardry quickly realize that he has that rarest quality found only in the very best teachers—the ability to intuit what every student needs, alternatively energizing the entire class or pulling aside a worried student for a chat and a cup of tea.

When I look at the faculty of Hogwarts, it is not Professor Lupin with whom I identify but the stern, no-nonsense professor of Transfiguration, Minerva McGonagall. Although Professor McGonagall is the head of Harry Potter's dormitory, she shows no favoritism and is not especially warm, something Harry and the other students find intimidating. If Professor McGonagall has a heart, she keeps it well-hidden—most of the time.

Harry and his friends Hermione and Ron respect Professor McGonagall and trust her—but they do not choose her as their confidant, nor do they try to fool her or manipulate her. They don't confuse her distance with dislike—in fact, they know that Professor McGonagall cares about them very much—but they don't want or need to hear her say any such thing.

I'm pretty sure that Professor McGonagall and I share this same characteristic, this way of letting our students know that we care by being the most demanding teachers we know how to be, expecting a great deal from our students and generally getting it. Each year I ask my seniors to anonymously evaluate my class and my teaching, and they consistently write that I am hard but fair, scary but fun. No one ever compliments me on my ability to hold a hand during a crisis. No one ever writes that I am sweet.

"Mrs. McSpadden, you are killing us with work," a student complained one time.

"Then you'll die educated," I said.

This sentiment prevails wherever students give me feedback. When I checked my school's listing on RateMy Teachers.com, a popular Web site in which students rate their teachers, I was delighted to have garnered a 5—the top score—for traits such as helpfulness and clarity. Most of my faculty also received high marks for being helpful or clear, but they also received high marks on "average easiness." In that category I received a 1—the lowest score possible, the only teacher to have done so.

Maybe to lessen the blow, one student evaluator added a note in the comment box.

"Mrs. McSpadden is difficult, but she knows her

material and she's one of those teachers who changes your outlook on life."

Nothing there about being sweet, or kind, or compassionate, or thoughtful, but that's okay. In another decade or so, the responsibilities of jobs and families will transfigure my students' memories of high school into something more mellow, and what once felt like hard work may look from the distance like a shiny treasure they found buried in the sand.

WORKING MIRACLES

November 15, 2000

THROUGH AN ODD JUXTAPOSITION of the calendar, American Education Week falls every year in November, which is also National Hospice Month. At first glance, these two disparate commemorations seem to have little in common. American Education Week, Nov. 12–18, is designed to celebrate the teachers who supported us and sent us into better lives. National Hospice Month is designed to raise awareness about an organization that supports us physically and emotionally when our lives are about to end.

This year, one teacher symbolizes for me the intimate connections between learning and dying.

She is swaddled in a dress several sizes too big, and her hair is chemotherapy thin, but her appearance isn't what sets her apart in the oncologist's office. Unlike everyone else who sits quietly reading or gazing into the distance, this woman is chatting with a man next to her, chatting in an upbeat, unwavering voice about a video she is planning on taping later with the help of her hospice nurse. The video, she tells her companion, is for her students. It is her last lesson plan.

"This way," she says, "they will know what is happening to me, and they will know what to expect if they come to see me."

She doesn't say what her prognosis is, but she doesn't need to—hospice steps in when death is on the horizon.

She doesn't say where she teaches or how old her students are, but they are lucky to have her, even as they are losing her.

My husband is also in that oncologist's office, but I'm not, my absence from this regular checkup a symbol of our hope that his year of follow-up treatment after colon cancer surgery has been successful, that every checkup from now on will be a minor interruption in an otherwise ordinary day.

Instead of offering a shoulder to lean on, I am at school teaching an ordinary lesson, even as the woman in the waiting room is planning her extraordinary one. In fact, I am watching a video with the entire student body in a darkened gym at my high school. The theme of this video is drug abuse and making good decisions, but I am paying indifferent attention until the face of Jane Smith flashes on the screen.

I recognize her immediately, even though I have seen her only once before. That was back in April when she was interviewed on the national news after donating one of her kidneys to Michael Carter, her eighth-grade student at Max Abbott Middle School in Fayetteville. Her generosity still takes my breath away, yet she is just as generous to her fellow teachers when she downplays her own sacrifice.

"Teachers try all the time to give their students a better life," she says, "This time a child just happened to come through who needed something other than unique instruction."

The video shows her walking with Michael in the hallway of their school. For the first time in years he is unchained from a dialysis machine; instead of an imminent death, he is facing a hopeful future.

That night when I tell my husband about Jane Smith's kidney donation, we both shake our heads in awe. When my husband tells me what he overheard at the doctor's office, we both weep at that teacher's determination to teach her students to the end, to show her students that the breadth of life need not be limited by its length.

These two teachers—the one in the oncologist's office and Jane Smith—may be the saints of my profession. Their generosity and courage stand in sharp contrast to my moments of impatience or selfishness in my classroom. Any smugness about my abilities as a teacher pales when I remember the lessons they have taught their students.

During this American Education Week, remember the adults in your life who greeted you at the school room door every day, who had interesting lessons planned and activities ready, who spent hours grading your assignments and tests and made you feel that what you had to say in class was worth hearing. Remember the teachers who noticed when you were sick or who understood when you forgot your homework, and remember those teachers who inspired equal measures of fear and respect and who refused to accept anything other than your best work.

Think of your life now—all the critical thinking skills you learned in someone's classroom, all the math and science and language you use every day that some teacher made sure you knew—and send one of those teachers a long-belated thank-you note.

Or tell your child's teacher that you are her partner, and ask what you can do to make her classroom more effective.

Or better yet, tell your own school-aged children and grandchildren what you have taken a lifetime to discover, that teachers really do try to make children's lives better. Send them to school with a positive attitude and the optimism that they can learn, and even those of us who aren't saints in the classroom might be able to work a few miracles.

A TEACHER REMEMBERED

April 28, 1999

I DIDN'T KNOW DAVE SANDERS, but like everyone else who read or watched the news from Columbine High School, I feel like I do now.

His bearded face has looked out from a line-up of the shooting victims. His colleagues and students have told the media stories of his devotion to his softball team and his business classes. He has been described as a popular teacher and dedicated coach.

I also saw a glimpse into his family when his grown daughters tearfully told of their young children's loss of a grandfather. Newspaper stories described how those two daughters were Dave's last view, their pictures in his wallet held in front of his eyes by his students as he bled to death on a classroom floor.

Dave Sanders' heroism as he shepherded frightened students away from the gunmen is extraordinary, but it is his ordinary courage as a teacher that interests me more. His decision to work with young people for 24 years signals his genuine concern about them. A teacher doesn't last for 24 years unless he is able to laugh with teenagers and find their youthful zest for life personally renewing.

I don't know what kind of teacher Dave Sanders was for all those years, but every good teacher spends enormous amounts of time planning for each class session, finding interesting and innovative ways to present the lessons, and evaluating the classes later. As a business teacher, he must have spent time and energy convincing students that vocational skills are valuable tools for them once they leave high school. He probably attended in-services on the changing job market so he could better tailor his courses to meet the needs of his students and their future employers. By necessity he spent hours of free time shackled to sets of papers to grade.

I don't know what kind of coach Dave Sanders was, but if he was like the coaches I know and work with, he knew the students in a way that is hard to achieve simply in the classroom. Those teachers who sacrifice their afternoons and weekends to direct a school play, assemble a yearbook, or coach a team see their students with more of their flaws and more of their charms. They spend part of their extracurricular contact teaching disappointed kids how to channel their losing streaks into determination to improve; they comfort the weary, listen to complaints, and celebrate the victories. Most of all they teach sportsmanship and maturity—qualities many students learn nowhere else but on a field or a stage after school. In his pictures with his softball team, Dave Sanders looks proud of his players, proud to be a coach of a girls team. The courage to face his team after a bitter loss or before a difficult practice is the courage I admire.

As his students begin their own courageous process of grieving for their loss of innocence, they will also have to put into perspective what they have lost with the death of Dave Sanders. Part of their grief work will include remembering the lessons he taught—the importance of hard work in the classroom and on the softball field. In his asides and stories to them he must have related his love for his family, and they watched him demonstrate the importance of that love as he held on with his gaze to those wallet photographs.

The image of Dave Sanders that haunts me most is the story his last students tell, of stripping off their tee shirts and pressing them to the bullet wounds in his shoulders, of desperately calling on their cell phones for help, of murmuring encouragement in their dying teacher's ear. My hope is that this final lesson—that despite our most heroic efforts we sometimes fail badly—will not be the lesson Dave Sanders' students remember best.

Dave Sanders' frantic protection of students under fire in the hall taught them that they were worth dying for; his presence in the halls every day before Tuesday taught them they were worth living for. That's the lesson I think Dave Sanders would wish for his legacy.

BACK TO SCHOOL

August 2, 2004

EVERY JUNE when school gets out, I go through a week of mourning the loss of my students. Time is purposeless and empty, and I'm adrift without an identity. As I gradually begin to catch up on my backlog of sleep and housework, my days become busy with neglected projects and urgent errands. I know I've made the transition to summer when I stop wondering why so many other people are out shopping or exercising at the Y or getting their cars fixed in the middle of the day.

For the next several weeks I am immeasurably rich. No more getting up before the sun.

No more stacks of essays to grade until midnight.

My sons get real breakfasts, not just bowls of stale cereal.

I read the paper over a second cup of coffee and plan what I will cook for lunch and supper.

The regular cashier at the McDonald's drive through wonders if I've moved away. Someone asks me if I would give up teaching and my students if I won the lottery.

In a heartbeat.

Then I blink twice and summer is over. While the heat is still shimmering on the asphalt, I get up and aim my car back to school for several in-service days packed with dull meetings and long waits at the copier. My grief at being back at work is every bit as intense as the grief I felt in June when I closed my classroom door and took home my empty briefcase. I dread the day the students return.

This year was no different. When my students returned last week, I winced for a moment at the noise in the halls, but then something odd began to happen as kids walked past my room and waved or called out. Students I have taught before ducked into my classroom for a quick hello before going to their new classes, and I was genuinely pleased to see them

The first day was full of rolls and books and routine housekeeping—but by the second day of class I started to remember why I love teaching teenagers. When my Advanced Placement English seniors came into my room, they found written on the board their first semester syllabus, a heavy schedule of reading that is intentionally intimidating. My students usually do fairly well on the end of the course AP exams, with most of them getting college credit as well as high school credit, but such success comes after a year of hard work, something I try to impress upon each class at the very beginning of school. This year's students looked suitably cowed as they wrote down their schedule of challenging books, though Tyler wasn't yet ready to let go of summer. He smirked and said, "Mrs. McSpadden, you have an assignment written on October 11th. You must not have known that October 11th is a national holiday."

"Oh?" I said with a raised eyebrow. "What is it? The celebration of your birth?"

Tyler laughed and said, "No! It's the first day of deer hunting season. Some of us won't be here that day."

Teaching in a rural school district, I've learned that whenever the absentee list is surprisingly long, some hunting season has just opened. Tyler was clearly giving me the heads-up about his planned day off.

"Well, Tyler," I said, eyebrow still raised, "I guess this year the deer will miss you."

Tyler grinned sheepishly, but his classmates howled when I added, "Of course, in the past, you missed the deer."

And there we were, teacher and students caught up in a vortex of friendly wisecracking and dizzy laughter, happy with each other's company. At last I was glad to be back.

That evening for the first time in many weeks, my family ate fast food. As usual during the school year I was too tired to cook, but even so, I hated giving up and heading to McDonald's this soon. Instead, I stopped by the take-out Chinese shop and placed an order. While I waited, a tiny dark-haired girl about six or seven years old watched me from behind the counter. Finally she asked, "Are you a teacher?"

I was flabbergasted. What had tipped her off? My scuffed, comfortable shoes? The mascara smudges under my eyes? A telltale smidgen of chalk or red ink?

"Yes, I'm a teacher," I told her. "How did you know?"

She looked me straight in the eye and said, "You look like one," in a tone suggesting she was dealing with a moron.

I have no idea what she saw, but when I carried my Chinese food out of the restaurant, I walked with a lighter step, a teacher—obviously—back in love with teaching and somehow broadcasting that to anyone perceptive enough to see it.

LESSONS
FROM HOME

SECOND CHANCES

February 28, 2004

MY PARENTS met in a leap year, which is probably a good thing.

They met at the lunch counter that my dad managed, refugees from first marriages that had ended badly. Their courtship was more of a cautious dance—one step reconnaissance, two steps retreat—than any romantic whirlwind.

To my dad, my mother was a striking brunette who refused to make eye contact when he refilled her coffee cup. Out of the corner of her eye my mother watched him berate the cooks and scold the waitresses, and she dubbed him "that hateful Charlie" to the other secretaries in her office.

She begged her friends to eat with her somewhere else on their lunch hour. Instead, they dragged her with them to the lunch counter and made small talk with Charlie while she blushed and looked away.

He wooed her slowly with free slices of yellow cake with chocolate buttercream frosting, with dishes of ice cream, with endless glasses of iced tea. Once he ran down the sidewalk after her as she headed back to her office and handed her a whole pie.

Still, she hesitated when he asked her to dinner and a movie. She was a divorced woman working and raising a daughter alone. Life was complicated enough.

Finally she relented, agreeing to meet him at her sister's house.

She was standing by the window when he drove up and stepped out of his car. As she watched the tall, wavy-haired man amble up the walkway, she may have had a premonition of what they would face if they ended up together: great financial hardship, a lifetime of backbreaking labor, the devastation of losing a son, the struggle to raise four daughters through the polarizing decades of the counterculture and Civil Rights Movement and Vietnam and Watergate. Her hand recoiled from the doorknob as she sensed the inevitable illnesses, the heart surgery, the broken hip, the incongruity of being young in old bodies.

"Tell him I'm not here," she told her sister suddenly, ducking into a back room. "Tell him to go away."

And he did, angrily.

I don't know when she saw him again. She doesn't know, either—"That was so long ago, Kay," my mother laughed when I asked her recently. All I know for certain is that they needed one more day to discover that they really were, as the saying goes, made for each other.

Let's imagine that the day is February 29, 1952, and for once my mother is not with her friends during their lunch hour. She has stayed behind in the office, lingering over some particularly troublesome bookkeeping while her friends head to the new diner several blocks away. Once she is sure they are gone, she gathers her coat and leaves, walking down the street to the department store. In the windows are posters Charlie has put up advertising turkey dinners for half a dollar, a bottomless cup of coffee for a nickel.

My mother walks past the department store and then turns around at the corner and heads back. Despite the chill her palms are sweaty when she pushes open the heavy door.

As she navigates through aisles of sewing notions and pots and pans, she sweeps her glance ahead, looking for Charlie. To her relief and disappointment she doesn't see him.

She slides onto a stool and picks up the small cardboard menu. Suddenly he is in front of her, coffee pot in hand. Always before, his scowls had been directed at his employees, but now he is frowning at her.

"Why did you do me that way?" he asks, and my mother shrugs and blushes. How can she tell this man what she herself doesn't know quite how to say, that loving someone requires more faith than she thinks she can muster?

Imagine then that she has another premonition, this time of riding joyfully from a day at the beach with little sunburned daughters licking ice cream cones in the back seat of a stifling hot car, or staying up all night on Christmas Eve putting together tricycles and bicycles and Barbie houses, or cooling off dozens of guests each July 4th with tin tubs of iced watermelons, or putting away the last washed dish before sitting down to watch another Thanksgiving football game. She looks up at Charlie, this man who might share these moments with her, and she says, "Everyone deserves a second chance."

Tomorrow—February 29—is a gift rarely given and less often appreciated. It is a reminder that a single day can make a difference in all the days which follow it. Tomorrow we can play it safe or take a risk—look at the world through someone else's eyes, offer a hand to someone lonelier than ourselves, love someone who needs a heart to share.

February 29—and every day—is a second chance to make things right.

LEGACIES

February 29, 2000

WHAT A DIFFERENCE a day makes.

In one day we realign the gradually slipping calendar to match the seasons; in one day we suffer tragedy or experience joy that marks who we are for the rest of our lives; in one day I decided that I would become a teacher.

On that day I was seven years old, a timid second grader enduring the unhappy autumn of Mrs. Bailey's teaching career. To my eyes she was ancient—gray-haired, stout, frowning, loud. Her favorite teaching strategy was screaming her displeasure.

She screamed at me the day I wept in frustration at the mysteries of the multiplication table. She screamed louder the day I forgot my lines as Queen Isabella in the Columbus Day pageant. She screamed when I was late finishing my assignments and when my classwork was crumpled, when I left my milk carton on the lunch table and when I spilled the contents of my satchel on the floor. I hated her even as I longed for her approval.

But the most shameful day—the one so dark that any happy moments are hidden in its shadows—was the day that I knew that I would be a teacher.

I was not the first child that day to be the target of Mrs. Bailey's anger, but by the time she turned her attention to me, she had worked herself into such a shrill yell that the first-grade teacher across the hall looked in the door. As Mrs. Bailey rained down her philippic on my chastened head, I cried hot tears into my lap and thought to myself, "I could do a better job than this. When I grow up, I'm going to be a teacher, and I won't make little children cry."

When I tell this story to my high school students, I usually end by saying, "And so I grew up to be a teacher who makes big children cry." We laugh since most of the time I am fairly even-tempered, certainly not a screamer, but once in awhile I feel Mrs. Bailey's presence hovering about the corners of my classroom when I do something that causes distress—such as springing a pop test after a difficult reading selection or assigning a demanding book over the Christmas holidays.

If Mrs. Bailey taught me that one day can be a contradiction of humiliation and resolve, another woman taught me the opposite, that a day can be a watershed of forgiveness and love.

This time I was 16, a timid new driver learning to navigate the narrow one-way streets of Charleston in my boxy '64 Ford. On this particular day I was in a hurry and backed out of our driveway at an awkward angle. The back right wheel slipped off the ledge into the ditch, tipping the car askew and levering the front left tire more than two feet off the ground, the nose of the car pointing to the sky. Somehow I managed to open the door and climb down, but I walked around in circles, shocked into nausea, too frightened to tell my mother what I had done.

Finally, however, I had to go back into the house and confess.

I never could have imagined what happened next. Instead of being angry with me, instead of scolding me for being careless, instead of resenting the trouble of calling a wrecker to lift the car back into the driveway—instead of any of the responses I could have foreseen, my mother conferred on me such a measure of absolution that I have never forgotten it.

"Oh," she said sympathetically, "I've always been afraid that would happen to me, too."

I wish I could say that with my own children and with my own students I have always been as understanding as my mother was with me that day, but that would be a lie. Some days I am too impatient, too eager for the afternoon bell, too generous with criticism and stingy with praise to be inspiring or inspired. But on those days when I remember that my students are someone's children—vulnerable, frightened at times, undervalued by a society that venerates entertainment above education—on those days I am able to be my mother's daughter.

One day doesn't seem long enough to matter in the course of an entire lifetime, but this quirky 29th day of February reminds us that every day is a chance to make a difference—in the slipping calendar, in our personal histories of pain and joy, in our decisions.

A day is sometimes even long enough to leave our legacies, good or evil, in the hearts and minds of the children in our care.

GIVING THANKS

November 23, 2003

As a child, I always thought that the day after Christmas was the dreariest day of the year. So much highflying anticipation before Christmas had to be balanced with a day of serious gravity. I was walking proof that Newton's law applied to children as well as apples—I had gone up, and now I had to come down.

Not so the day after Thanksgiving. The interlude between the best kid holiday—Halloween—and Thanksgiving was spent relatively quietly. At school we listened to the familiar tale of the first Thanksgiving and colored pictures of somber Pilgrims, mildly annoyed that our black crayons—the only ones needed—were worn down from earlier cats, bats, witches, and cauldrons.

The day itself was rather slow with easy kitchen chores—setting out pickles and olives while the adults wrestled the turkey and beat the potatoes.

My sister and I watched the parades on TV and strolled around in the afternoon with uncomfortably stuffed bellies, bored and not particularly thankful, while the adults napped on the couches, getting up their strength to begin the frenzy of holiday shopping that started when the stores opened the next day. No one had time to feel let down the day after Thanksgiving. No one even remembered Thanksgiving. Christmas was coming!

This rush from holiday to holiday bothered me when I was a child. I used to try to keep the holidays distinct and memorable through force of will, saying, "I will remember this!" like a mantra. No matter how hard I looked at everything around me, no matter how elevated my feelings, I couldn't hold on to them for very long.

Thanksgiving was the hardest to hold on to. Gratitude is hard to sustain, though I'm not sure I ever really felt gratitude as a child, not in the mature meaning of accepting our indebtedness to others. Oh, I often said thank you, but what I felt was glad, not grateful. The kind of gratitude called for at Thanksgiving is something else, something that comes only after we have suffered and reflected on that suffering. Real gratitude means accepting our limitations as we acknowledge our dependence on each other. It is hard work for someone like me who imagines herself capable and autonomous.

Last week when my seniors and I were reading Wordsworth's *Lines Composed a Few Miles Above Tintern Abbey,* I was able to recapture—briefly—the gratitude I felt the first time I read this poem. Exactly thirty years ago my senior English teacher, Audrey Smoak, read *Tintern Abbey* to us. Miss Smoak was loving and stern, judgmental and forgiving, intimidating and friendly, and her students adored her.

That day I shivered when she read to us and I realized that Wordsworth spoke for me, describing my own attempts to hold on to memories:

> *in this moment there is life and food*
> *For future years.*

Wordsworth wrote about his walking tour through the Wye Valley. He wanted to reassure his sister, his companion on the trip, that their journey together would remain important to him, that he would find it a source of comfort when he was back home in the city.

Tintern Abbey is not Wordsworth's most accessible poem—it is unrhymed, long, in turns rapturous and philosophical—but Miss Smoak read with such feeling and meaning that I scribbled notes in both margins of the textbook I still use. She has been dead for years—dying young and painfully of spinal cancer—but I heard her voice again when I read to my own students. "Think of some examples to illustrate this," I said to them, and I read:

> *feelings too*
> *Of unremembered pleasure: such, perhaps,*
> *As have no slight or trivial influence*
> *On that best portion of a good man's life,*
> *His little, nameless, unremembered, acts*
> *Of kindness and of love.*

My students were quick to offer examples. They spoke of strangers who helped them gather up dropped books in the busy hallway, salesclerks who directed them to better deals, fellow drivers who stopped a line of traffic to let them turn left. They spoke of people they knew and people they didn't know whose unexpected gifts had landscaped their world with beauty. They agreed that we rarely feel enough gratitude, that we are the beneficiaries more often than the benefactors of good deeds.

Wordsworth isn't clear whether he refers to the "little, nameless acts of kindness and love" that are performed for us or which we perform for others. I'm glad. This way the poem isn't just a nudge to do good works, but is also a reassurance that in the end, nothing is lost, nothing is really forgotten.

During the rush of another holiday season, I find that comforting. I may not be able to consciously hold on to my feelings of peace and gratitude in the whirlwind of cooking and cleaning and shopping and traveling, but those feelings provide some counterweight and keep me grounded, even when I am unaware.

A MOTHER'S POWER

July 2, 2005

DEAR MAMA,

I have no way to thank you for the big things you have given me—life, health, a happy childhood—but as you prepare to celebrate your 80th birthday this July 4, I offer a few words of gratitude for the small gifts you have given that in retrospect haven't been so small after all.

Thank you for playing dumb around your children, for letting us believe that we were geniuses whose mother apparently knew next to nothing. No matter what we had learned at school that day, you had never heard of it.

"Napoleon? Who was he? Tell me about him. Zambia? Where is that? What are the people like there? Brushing your teeth up and down is better than side to side? Who knew," you said. Ah, your obvious pleasure when I taught you something! Did you know that you were giving me the joy of being a teacher at the tender age of seven?

Thank you for herding my younger sister Darlene and me into the kitchen to clean up after every meal. If we complained, you painted a picture of the misery of a sink of dishes lurking beneath water cold and greasy. Better to attack them right away, you would say, and feel the relief of being truly free. Even now when I am tempted to give in to procrastination, I hear your voice urging me onward.

Thank you for being too tired to finish reading a single bedtime story.

"Here, Kay," you would say in the middle of *Snow White* or *Cinderella*, yawning. "I'm just too sleepy. You read the rest to Darlene."

And the three of us would snuggle close in the bed as I practiced a priceless skill. In my classroom today I sometimes hook my struggling readers the same way, reading aloud enough of the story to gain their attention, making the finish line of The End within reach.

Thank you for turning a deaf ear when I complained about having to learn to sew, to type, to cook, to play the piano.

"I don't need this stuff!" I whined, but you wisely ignored me. When the children in my own life—my sons, my students—make similar complaints, I don't argue but I do insist, the way you did.

Thank you for punishing me less and absolving me more than I deserved, for believing that the spirit of the law was more important than the letter, for bending the rules on occasion and making my childish heart jubilant with a Coke at bedtime, an extra dessert, another hour of TV.

Thank you for giving me "advances" on my allowance knowing I'd never repay them, proving to me that mercy is better than justice.

Thank you for proudly wearing the cheap perfume and gaudy costume jewelry I bought you, letting me know that a mother's love is larger than her need for style.

Thank you for showing me that mothers prefer the chicken wing, the burned cookie, the heel of the bread.

Thank you for holding me close when I needed to be held, and for letting me face the world on my own when I was ready.

In many ways the world hasn't changed enough since you were born in 1925. That was the year the Geneva Protocols called for banning weapons of mass destruction; eight decades later we are no safer. In 1925 40,000 KKK members marched in Washington; in 2005 the Klan is still in the news as Edgar Ray Killen is tried at last. You were barely a week old when the Scopes trial began, and the debate over teaching evolution rages on.

In other ways the world has been shaken by tremendous change. You lived through the century which saw the Great Depression, bloody wars, political strife, race riots, advances in technology which have proven both a blessing and a curse.

And you have stepped into a century which began with a celebration but which has already devolved into violence and bitter culture wars.

Still, you tell me not to despair. Life is too short to worry, you say. Things tend to work out in the end.

So thank you most for the gift of optimism, for refusing to obsess about what you can't change, for changing what you can, for enduring in the face of overwhelming sorrow, for pressing forward with your quiet courage, and for making me believe in the power of love.

GRACES

January 1, 2005

WHEN I WAS A CHILD, the Christmas gift that offered the most promise—and the greatest disappointment—was a diary. Over the years I received several of these small leather-bound books, and my arc of experience with them never varied.

From Christmas until New Year's I would open the diary every day, smoothing my palm over the first blank page and pondering how I would initiate my life story. The diary would soon be filled with the amazing details of my life, details so weighted with significance that they had to be kept behind lock and key. For the next 365 days the diary would be my own little Stonehenge highlighting the solstices of my childhood.

At least that was my intention. Part of the problem of the diary was evident from the first entry on—I had nothing much to say. Although my life felt full and fun, when

I tried to record it ("Today I went to school" or "Tonight we had meatloaf for supper") it became what it really was, the bare bones of a life so ordinary that it bored even me to reread it. The tiny lock and key, once the most appealing part of the diary, became superfluous. I had no secrets worth hiding.

Another problem with the diary was deciding on an audience. Was I writing it for me, for some future self to read with bemusement? If I grew up and got married, would I show it to my husband some day, or my children? Should I tell them hello from the past? And what if I became a famous pianist or a champion roller skater, two careers I often contemplated? Would a museum beg to display my childish diary in a protective glass case, perhaps opening to February 12 ("This morning I went to the rink and practiced my salchow. After a meatloaf supper at home I practiced my Beethoven sonata") as evidence that hard work really does pay off?

For the first week of January, and sometimes even into the second week, I was a diligent diarist. I chronicled my activities and memorialized my thoughts. Then a day might pass without comment, followed by a frantic rededication, but inevitably my interest would flag and I would skip more and more days until I abandoned the diary altogether. The last time I received a diary for Christmas I did not get past January 1.

"Today I started my new diary," I wrote, and the stupid obviousness of that statement so disgusted me that I threw the diary into a toy chest in my parents' garage where it stayed until years later the floods of Hurricane Hugo consigned it to the landfill with other unloved trash.

Every January 1 I think of my early failures with my diaries. The first day of a new year cries out for special recognition—the year ahead lies as fresh and blank as the pages of a diary. I still long to quarter my life into neatly organized blocks, to assert control and say to a large, seemingly indifferent universe, "This you may do, but that I will not allow."

This week has been full of lessons about our illusions of control. The earth slips and thousands of people are crushed under houses or swept out to sea. Another car explodes in Baghdad. A snow storm turns lethal. A doctor tells a young father that he has no more experimental cancer treatments to replace the ones that haven't worked. Go home and enjoy the holidays, the doctor says, and the father hears what the words really mean.

But even in the midst of the chaos and pain we have had moments of unexpected grace and beauty—the delight of a child, the embrace of a loved one, a gift chosen with care and received with appreciation. Not just the bare bones of our lives, but the muscle and matter, too, the things that written in a diary seem spare but in real life give us meaning and hope.

Grace happens in the corner of our eye, when our attention is directed elsewhere, when we are not looking for it. It happens when we stop forcing our will on others with a rigid hand, when we open our fist and hold our palm upward to catch the rain. It happens after the storm of intense grief has shaken us, when we are quiet inside, when we think we have lost it forever.

Grace is the lesson waiting to be discovered every new year when we throw away the diary. It is a blank page, luring us forward into possibility.

THE HOOTSIE DAISY HIGHWAY

WFAE April 2, 2002

ONE SPRINGTIME several years ago when my younger son, Will, was 10 or 11 years old, we were driving past some open pastureland when we noticed fields of wildflowers and rows of daffodils blooming alongside the road.

"I learned something interesting this week in social studies about wildflowers," Will said. "Want to hear it?"

"No," his older brother replied with the kind of knee-jerk refusal necessary for keeping younger brothers in subordination. "Nobody wants to hear what you learned."

But I did. We had already been driving for quite some time and I was tired. My job on those long trips was to be the family storyteller, and I had exhausted my cache of fairy tales, plots from Shakespeare, and stories from *Don Quixote* and *The Canterbury Tales*.

I had retold all the American short stories that I knew and had even recounted great chunks of novels which I could barely remember. A sixth grade social studies lesson was a welcomed relief.

"A long time ago in the 1830's," Will began, "there was this slave in Georgia named Hootsie. Her master was really cruel to her, beating her and starving her, and one day she decided to run away."

"What does that have to do with flowers?" his brother snorted.

"You'll see," Will said, and then he continued. "The night before Hootsie left Georgia, she sneaked into the shed where the master kept his tools and stuff, and she took two old buckets and filled them up with flower seeds. Then as she ran away, she threw out handfuls of seeds behind her so that when spring came, the other slaves would see a path to freedom."

"Sort of a cross between Johnny Appleseed and Harriet Tubman," I said, and Will agreed.

"That path of flowers became known as the Hootsie Daisy Highway, and you can still see parts of it," Will told us. "They have historical markers along the way that tell the story."

The car hummed forward and I was caught up in Will's description of the brave slave woman. I could imagine the night she slipped quietly towards the shed, tree frogs and crickets and an occasional dog shattering the silence, the creaking of the door, the damp earth beneath her feet, her hands scooping out flower seeds and storing them in oak buckets.

We drove past another large field of white and yellow

daisies and I wondered if they might be the descendants of Hootsie's long-ago flowers. "You know," I said, "a couple of buckets of seeds wouldn't go very far. What did Hootsie do when she ran out?"

Will was busy looking out the window but he answered right away. "When Hootsie ran out of seeds, she would always stop and ask people for more. All those people on the Underground Railroad who gave her a place to hide would give her more seeds for her journey. That's why the Hootsie Daisy Highway goes all the way from Georgia to Wyoming."

"Wyoming!" I asked, and Will said, "Wyoming, Wisconsin, some state with a W."

I glanced in the rearview mirror and caught his grin.

He was laughing, and the lovely metaphor of a path of flowers to freedom shimmered and faded into the fiction it was.

"You mean, there really aren't any historical markers?" I asked, reluctant to let go of the image of the courageous slave. "You mean you made up the Hootsie Daisy Highway?"

Will nodded proudly, and I knew that I had lost my place as the family storyteller.

SEASONS

June 22, 2002

SINCE SUMMER BEGAN, I have had a twinge in my lower back, quite possibly from lugging so many watermelons from my car to my kitchen. Every three or four days I have returned to the store to buy another one, each one sweet and juicy and quickly eaten.

I worry that my family will tire of watermelons, but my 13-year-old son assures me that he won't. After all, what is summer for except to eat truly ripe fruit? Summer means locally-grown strawberries and peaches, blueberries that are still plump, blackberries plucked from roadside hedges. In the winter I make do with autumn apples and grapes grown in South America, but warm weather brings different flavors to the table.

One day when my son and I drive to the local fruit stand to buy yet another watermelon, suddenly he says, "You were right when you said I don't want to grow up."

His words are an invitation to continue a conversation we had started weeks ago, right after school ended for the summer. He had wept then on the last day of eighth grade, and though I reminded him that he had never really enjoyed middle school, he was inconsolable.

I had told him that high school was a chance to make new friends, learn new skills. He told me that the devil you know is often more appealing than the one lurking in the future.

"Perhaps," I had finally suggested, "the real problem is that you don't want to have to grow up."

At the time he hadn't answered—he had concentrated on his Gameboy instead—but he has obviously been thinking.

"I want to stay young," he says now as we drive to the fruit stand. "I like being this age."

I glance at him in the rearview mirror and catch a quick glimpse of his face. He doesn't look like someone who is enjoying anything at the moment. He looks like a boy wrestling with misery.

"Well," I say, "every age has its own pleasures. Surely you wouldn't want to miss out on the fun of being an adult."

He scoffs.

"What's so good about being an adult?" he asks, and I say, "Having children, having a job that you really enjoy, getting to do things to help other people instead of always being the one who needs to be taken care of."

He's quiet, and I wonder if I really mean what I have

told him. Is being an adult better than being a child? I think of the past two decades of my own life, years blessed by children, by a fulfilling job as a teacher, with a husband and friends and projects, but also with arthritic knees and reading glasses and dreams that had to be set free from possibility.

"I'm glad you like being the age you are," I tell my son. "I don't want you to grow up too fast. But I like being the age I am, too."

"You always give me good advice, Mom," my son says without a trace of sarcasm. I drive on smugly.

Later, when I am slicing peaches for a cobbler and cutting up the watermelon, I stop feeling so smug when I realize that my homegrown wisdom isn't so homegrown after all. I have plagiarized this idea straight from the Old Testament book of Ecclesiastes.

"To everything there is a season," Ecclesiastes declares, and I decide that instead of being a text about fatalism and the inevitable changes we face, the words are a celebration of now, of savoring the fruit available only in the summer, of cherishing the safety of eighth grade. "To everything there is a season" is justification for scorning unnatural hothouse tomatoes and waiting for the ones that ripen in July, the flavor more intense because it is rare. "To everything there is a season" is encouragement to sleep in on Saturdays, to call a friend when we are lonely, to learn to play an instrument during retirement.

It is not a rationale for self-indulgence, but a call to appreciation. Life is seasonal, the writer of Ecclesiastes reminds us, and each season has its own peculiar joys and sorrows.

I don't know if my son will find any comfort in these words this fall when he starts high school, but whether he wants to or not, he will have to grow up someday. He may enjoy his teenaged years, or he may simply endure them, but either way, they won't last forever.

In the meantime, for as long as summer lasts, I plan to feed him plenty of watermelon.

DRIVING

WFAE February 5, 2002

TEACHING A TEENAGER to drive is exactly like the old description of war: long hours of boredom punctuated by a few moments of terror. Recently I have been teaching my son to drive, spending what feels like hours hunched in the passenger side of the car while he careens around corners just a bit too quickly or accelerates under yellow lights just a bit too slowly. Being his teacher has brought out the worst in me, and in addition to teaching him some driving skills, I have taught him that his mother occasionally uses words she shouldn't even know.

However, his progress has been slow but sure, and as we get nearer to the day for the actual driver's test, my son spends his practice time preparing for that most fearsome of hurdles for young drivers, parallel parking. His high school has even set up parallel barriers at one end of the parking lot, and on weekends, cars sometimes line up to use them.

One afternoon, my son is driving me dizzy in circles in the high school lot as he pulls up to the barriers, backs up, parks, and pulls out for another try. As we circle around again and again, I notice that a young father has parked his van nearby and is lifting his daughter's tiny pink bike from the hatch. His daughter looks three or four years old, too small to be able to ride, but as soon as her father buckles on her helmet, she straddles the bike and takes off, never looking back, her father watching her speed away.

For a moment as my son swings our Honda around for yet another try at parallel parking, I meet the gaze of the father. Something uneasy stirs inside him as he knows that one day he will be here in my place, bored in the passenger seat, his daughter a pretty 16-year-old badgering him to let her get her license, and he will not like it. The shadowy memory of this afternoon and her tiny bike—her first independent wheels—will make him feel unaccountably sad, reminding him that his daughter is growing up, growing away, but he will shake that feeling off and feel, instead, pride at her maturity and her accomplishment.

I know that father will feel this, because I feel it now. The hazy, long-ago images of my own son and his first small, blue bike sting, somehow, but I chase them away by stealing a glance at the 16-year-old driver beside me, his 6'4" frame folded stiffly into the seat, his concentration on the parallel barrier steady and determined.

And I know something else, too—that both that father and I have worked so hard to launch our children

KAY McSPADDEN

into independence without quite realizing what we have done. Our children will one day be masters of the road, will fly all over the world, will know how to buy a bus ticket or ride a commuter train. Their world will move quickly with them, and when we nag them to come home for a visit, they will remind us of the speed of their lives.

If we are lonely then, we will have only ourselves to blame.

LEAVING

September 24, 2004

WHEN MY 18-YEAR-OLD SON Jamie was still a wee lad of five or six, he polished off his french fries with gusto and asked for more.

"Here's the money to buy some," I told him, pointing to the counter where several teenagers in Burger King uniforms were standing idle. "Walk up there and tell one of those people you want an order of fries."

Jamie is a natural introvert who balked at the idea of speaking to a stranger.

"You do it," he said, pushing the money back into my palm.

It was one of those awful moments when a good mother would have intuitively understood her son's reticence and even embraced it as central to his shy nature. A good mother—I thought later—would have squeezed her son's shoulder reassuringly, leaned close to his ear and said, "That's okay, honey. I'll walk with you and stand beside you while you order your fries. Mama will be right there."

A good mother would have found a loving, empathetic way to help her son.

A good mother would have been hard to find in Burger King that day.

"If you want french fries you are going to have to go get them yourself," I said. "You have to stop being so afraid of things!" Then I handed him the money and gave him a little shove. He tucked his head down and walked to the counter like a man going to his own execution. Finally he looked back at me, his eyes wide and imploring.

"Go on!" I waved dismissively. "Unless you don't want those fries."

I've returned to that scene many times lately, especially the part where I gave him a push and said, "Go."

I may have pushed too hard.

A month ago my husband and I drove for two days to take Jamie to the foreign world of New England where he began his freshman year at Yale. On the way we passed several fine institutions of higher education where he could have matriculated but which, in the end, he judged too comfortable, too familiar, too close to home.

Instead we took him to a college with ancient buildings and tiny dorm rooms (7 by 11 feet for two large boys!). We warned him that the winters would be brutal, that the people might not be kind, that his Southern accent and public school education and blue-collar Scots-Irish heritage might be social handicaps. Once we had unloaded our car, we got ready for the two-day drive home like people going to our own executions. We looked at our son with wide and imploring eyes.

"Don't worry about me," he said, hugging us at the gate and waving us into the line of traffic. "Go."

Since then we have heard from him often, most of his e-mails and phone calls saying the same thing in different words: "I'm happy! Don't miss me!"

Serves me right, I guess, my hand on his back all those years ago still metaphorically giving him permission to leave.

My husband was not at the Burger King that day. He would have been that compassionate parent who took his son by the hand and bought him a milkshake to go with the fries. He was the parent who once, looking down into the face of his sleeping newborn, wept bitterly, saying, "I can't believe he is going to grow up one day and leave us."

Leaving and returning are themes that shake us profoundly in literature as well as in our lives. Perhaps no book deals with them better than Homer's *Odyssey*, the first book I read each school year with my seniors. This ancient story about Odysseus' return from the Trojan War has many obvious parallels to the lives of my students. Like Odysseus, they are on a journey. Like him, they have adventures ahead.

But unlike him, they are more concerned with leaving than with returning. They are like his son, Telemachus, whose story is in many ways the interesting one. At the beginning of *The Odyssey* Telemachus is a victim of opportunists, unsure of himself, scared. Then the goddess Athene tells him to embark on a journey of his own. Grow up, she tells him. Get off your duff and see what you can learn.

By coincidence, Jamie is also reading *The Odyssey* in a class at Yale. After I told him recently that his dad, in particular, was missing him, he referred to it in a letter:

"I still love Yale. It feels a lot like home now. However, last night I found this passage in *The Odyssey* when I was reading: *So nothing is as sweet as a man's own country, his own parents, even though he's settled down in some luxurious house off in a foreign land and far from those who bore him.* Maybe home is still 'sweet' although I have 'settled down' in the 'luxurious house' that is Yale. Odysseus thinks that one's own country and parents are still better. Perhaps this is true in my case, too."

Go. Learn. We're there with you after all.

INTIMATIONS OF MORTALITY

August 13, 2005

I HADN'T HEARD FROM DAVID in 29 years, but when he phoned the other night I could immediately picture him— his mop of dark curls, his wire-framed glasses, his goofy smile. As English majors at the same college we sometimes took classes together or waved to each other in the halls. We occasionally shared a meal in the cafeteria or talked about the books we were reading when we bumped into each other at the student union. David was funny and silly and anxious, too, in an endearing way.

Perhaps his performance in his church's Christmas pageant best illustrates this. When David was a teenager in high school he was cast as Joseph. He and the other teens persuaded the minister that they knew the Christmas story so well that they could ad lib their lines instead of wasting time rehearsing. The pageant went fine at first— the announcing angel spoke clearly, the shepherds acted suitably afraid. Then David-Joseph knocked loudly on the innkeeper's door and asked for a room.

"Sorry," the innkeeper said. "We're booked up."

"But my wife's pregnant!" David-Joseph pleaded.

"That's not my fault," the innkeeper quipped, and David-Joseph wailed, "It's not my fault either!"

When he called recently he was still funny and kind, but more mature, too, and not at all silly or anxious. He had seen my name in an alumni magazine and wanted to reconnect.

"So tell me what you have been doing for 29 years," he said, and I was horrified that I could sum up my life in a single sentence.

"I got married, had children, and have been working. What about you?"

David told me about his teaching, his graduate work, his family. And then he mentioned, almost as an aside, that he is dying.

"It's progressive, and it's terminal," he said. "I've stopped asking 'why me?' Why not me?"

I wasn't sure what to say, but David seemed comfortable with my stumbled condolences.

"I'm past being angry," he said. "I don't have time to be angry."

And then he changed the subject, asking me details about my husband, my children, my job. He remembered the name of my college roommate and asked about her. Sheepishly I admitted that I had let her slip out of my life a decade ago.

"And our other friends?" David asked. "The ones we knew from the campus ministry programs?"

But there I failed him, too. I had not kept in touch with a single one of our mutual friends.

If David was disappointed in me, he did not show it. Only later did I realize that David's call was prompted by his sense of urgency. Not quite a believer in my own mortality, I have allowed friendships to lapse in a way David no longer can.

Letting things slide—believing I have forever—is how I operate most of the time, not with the good humor and clear-eyed grace that David seems to have.

Earlier this summer I was offered a brief reminder of mortality when my family took a tour through the Civil War battlefield of Gettysburg. My husband and I were already feeling a little sad that our child-rearing years are ending as our younger son enters his last year of high school and our time with him is winding down.

Driving slowly across the landscape where 51,000 men died or were wounded in three days in July 1863 and walking over the even sadder landscape of unmarked graves in the cemetery, we were somber and silent. The men who died there—many of them boys my son's age— were not even able to summarize their lives as I had thoughtlessly summarized my own: "I got married, I had children, I worked."

"You seem to have had a nice life," David had said on the phone, shaming me that a dying man had to remind me to be grateful.

Before David and I hung up, we exchanged addresses and promised to write. I think I'll let him know that his role as Joseph has become part of our annual Christmas lore. I may send him a poem or two, or perhaps just some of the last lines from Matthew Arnold's elegant poem about loss, "Dover Beach."

> Ah, love, let us be true
> To one another! for the world, which seems
> To lie before us like a land of dreams,
> So various, so beautiful, so new,
> Hath really neither joy, nor love, nor light,
> Nor certitude, nor peace, nor help for pain.

Staring into the abyss of loss is never easy, but Arnold mitigates the sorrow with the reassurance that our love for each other makes the suffering bearable. David's call reminded me of the importance of our connection to each other and the roles we all play in each other's living and in our dying.

HOLIDAYS

October 8, 2005

MY FATHER LOVES HOLIDAYS more than anyone I know. When I was growing up, Halloween and Christmas were of seismic proportions, requiring weeks of planning and decorating. Easter meant putting up a wall-size poster of a bunny and dyeing dozens of eggs. Labor Day meant stoking up the grill and inviting all the neighbors for a cookout. We celebrated Sadie Hawkins Day, no less, with a greased climbing pole and a race.

Even birthdays became holidays. Every May my father threw himself a huge birthday party, and when our own birthdays rolled around, he invited all our friends and treated us to parties at the skating rink.

When my first son, Jamie, was born, I continued my father's tradition and celebrated each birthday with gusto. One year we set up the backyard with treasures to find in a scavenger hunt. Another year we let the guests decorate and bake their own pizzas and cookies. More than once our house became Hogwarts School of Witchcraft and Wizardry and the guests made magic wands and played an earthbound version of Quidditch.

Last year Jamie's 19th birthday was the first one he had ever had without his family nearby to help him celebrate. He didn't seem to mind—he was, after all, busy with his first year of college—but I arranged with a bakery near the university to have a large cake delivered to his dorm room. When he called later that night to thank me, he assured me that the cake was delicious—and he made me promise never to do anything like that again.

Soon I'll be able to buy him a piece of cake and watch him eat it in person. Parents Weekend coincides with Jamie's 20th birthday, and although I had not planned to go this year, he asked his dad and me to be there.

Going is stressful. Leaving town means crafting lesson plans that a substitute teacher can follow well enough so that my students don't lose instructional time. It means making sure my younger son has enough food in the fridge, gas in his car, and an alarm clock that works. It means buying plane tickets and paying exorbitant hotel fees. It means rushing to pack and leaving things behind—always. I've been frustrated and resentful this week instead of happily anticipating Jamie's birthday.

My father would not approve.

And then the other morning I opened the paper and saw what all teachers eventually see if they teach long enough. One of my recent students had died. The article about him read like a short tragic poem.

Alcohol.

Speeding.

No seat belt.

Coming home from a late night birthday party.

19 years old.

His mother's only child.

In his poem "Auto Wreck," Karl Shapiro explains our response to such a senseless loss this way:

> *But we remain, touching a wound*
> *That opens to our richest horror.*
> *Already old, the question Who shall die?*
> *Becomes unspoken Who is innocent?*
> *For death in war is done by hands;*
> *Suicide has cause and stillbirth, logic;*
> *But this invites the occult mind,*
> *Cancels our physics with a sneer,*
> *And spatters all we knew of denouement*
> *Across the expedient and wicked stones.*

I've lost students to accidents, to suicide, to murder, and each death is a violation of the expected chronology of the world. We freight our children with memories of our time with them and hope that they carry us forward into their futures. When they don't—when they can't—a part of ourselves dies, too, and we grieve our own mortality even as we weep for the loss of such a young life.

I've stopped whining about Parents Weekend. My students will be fine without me. My younger son can handle a weekend at home alone without being bailed out by Mom. I can survive a few days with whatever I'm doomed to forget to pack, and when I get back and the credit card bill comes, I'll bite my tongue and pay it without complaint.

After all, this may be the last birthday that Jamie and I spend together. Even if we both live long, full lives, we may live them apart, and the people just over his horizon—his friends and colleagues, the family he will create—are the ones who will share his future celebrations.

I hope he will prove himself his grandfather's heir and celebrate every holiday, big and small, and every birthday, too, long and loud. But even more, I hope he celebrates all the days in between and recognizes what gifts they really are.

EMPTY NESTS

I USED TO LIVE IN AN EMPTY NEST. My husband, Randy, and I were married for seven years before we had our first child, years when our most detailed conversations involved what to do for the weekend. Would we see a new movie? Go to a new restaurant? Stay home and stay up late watching old *Star Trek* reruns on TV? I filled my leisure time with trying out new cookbooks, working gigantic jigsaw puzzles, entering trivia contests, sleeping late on Saturdays. When I won tickets to a Leo Kottke concert, we immediately decided to go. We had no idea who Leo Kottke was, but the tickets were free and so were we.

For at least a year after our first son, Jamie, was born, Randy and I looked like shell-shocked prisoners of war. Gone were the useless cookbooks, the child-choking jigsaw puzzles, the ability to remember trivia, time for sleep. Gone, indeed was any leisure at all.

And then, just when Jamie was old enough to talk intelligibly and sleep through the night, we did it again.

"This is your baby," we told Jamie the day we brought our younger son, Will, home, and we meant it. I had wanted a second baby because I had enjoyed having siblings, but Jamie was more skeptical. After several hours of enduring oohs and ahhs over the new baby, Jamie marched to the front door and announced that he was leaving.

And then a few years later he really did. Now his baby brother is all grown up, too, and this week he took flight, heading to college and his own adventures.

In some ways, having children has been like a roller coaster ride that looked a lot tamer from the ground. It was a shorter ride, too, than I expected, and not one that I particularly want to get off.

Not everyone I know feels the same way, of course. At a school open house several years ago, I recognized one mother because I had taught three of her five children, and her youngest son was in my senior English class.

"I know you must be sad that the empty nest is almost here," I said, and she scoffed.

"Huh!" she said. "I've been raising children for 34 years. I can't wait for this nest to be empty!"

You'd think I'd learn, but I said almost the same thing to another mother this week, one whose only child was leaving in a few days.

"I'm trying not to be sad," she told me, "because she's ready to leave. This is an exciting time for her, so I'm excited, too."

That seems to be one of the great truths about parenting, that a child's happiness completely mitigates the suffering or sacrifice a parent makes.

Unfortunately, another great truth is what worries me. A child's unhappiness multiplies the suffering and helplessness of a parent.

When Jamie left for college two years ago, he happily settled in and I stopped feeling anxious about him right away. Only when Will assures me that he is having a good time testing his own wings will I be able to relax.

At least children heading off today have an easier time letting their parents share their distant lives than we did years ago. In fact, *Newsweek* recently published an article that concluded that the Baby Boomers have a closer, more intimate relationship with their children than their parents had with them. Through the convenience of cell phones and e-mails, the Boomers' children stay connected as they head off to college or into the work force.

Until I read the article, I had smugly congratulated myself that Jamie was unusually thoughtful and emotionally close to us since we hear from him several times a week.

"According to *Newsweek*," I told him in an e-mail, "the children of the Baby Boomers are talking to their parents an average of ten times a week. That makes you a slacker!"

All that communication does help the nest feel less empty. On the other hand, I have fond memories of how cozy an empty nest can be. I've even bought two tickets to the Leo Kottke concert in September, hopeful that some music might help drive away any loneliness and sadness of a house newly silent.

But I also know that a house where children used to be is quieter than a house where no children ever were. Our children have touched us as if they had tossed a stone into our hearts, freighting us with the ache of overwhelming love and worry. Their presence, and their absence, ripples through us like waves on a pond. We are never truly still again.

YOUTH

KIDS TODAY

March 27, 2004

THE YEAR I BEGAN TEACHING, a retiring teacher took me aside to give me what she thought was sage advice.

"These kids today," she said, "are different from the ones I used to teach years ago. These kids don't respect anyone. They don't want to learn. I would quit now if this year was my first."

Fortunately—or perhaps, unfortunately—I am a hardheaded skeptic who has always preferred testing things for myself, so I didn't quit after that very difficult first year. I did indeed have disrespectful, indifferent students, but I also had many more students who were willing to learn and willing to teach me how to teach them. Teaching was very hard, but it was also great fun.

That was 27 years ago, and students haven't changed. Every year I struggle with a few disrespectful, indifferent teenagers, though I am able to forge peace treaties with most of them. The majority of my high school students are really good sports, willing to accept learning as an adventure and me as their travel guide. As the years have passed and I've begun teaching the children of former students, I become more convinced that the retiring teacher was wrong. Fashions may change quickly, and cultures may change gradually, but human nature seems set in stone.

Recently a reader sent me a wonderful gift of a book published by a teacher in 1939 which confirms this perception. Mary Ellen Chase in *A Goodly Fellowship* describes a group of working class children living on the coast of Maine in 1906 this way: "School to most of them was a necessary evil, alleviated only by recess and by the stories I told or read to them for two hours on Friday afternoons as a reward for good behavior. Few of them saw any present pleasure or any step toward the future." Despite the difficulties with overcrowding and few supplies, Chase learned to love her students and, in her own words, grew up that year.

She left Maine to teach in several other public schools, including Hillside, a boarding school designed by Frank Lloyd Wright and run by Ellen and Jane Lloyd-Jones, his aunts. From them she learned that "learning is never dull, that only dull teachers make it so."

Chase embraces this attitude in her summary of good teaching when she writes, "I have learned that my methods must be as different and varied as the different and varied personalities of my students, who from the start are governed by forces over which I have small control. I have learned that to know precisely what I am doing in any given class at any given moment is a state of mind as intolerably dull for my students as for myself."

She goes on to specifically address teaching English and its role in developing critical thinking skills.

"It is, then, this very necessity for elasticity of mind on the part of the teacher, for quick and intelligent changes in approach, which makes the teaching of English such a difficult job. We deal with the most personal and most fortified of possessions, with thoughts and feelings, suggestions and impressions, notions, fancies, predilections, ideas. We learn, if we are any good at our work, to welcome opposition, opinions different from our own, heresies, heterodoxies, iconoclasms. Our delight lies in the activity of awakened minds....Our aim is to intensify the powers of thinking and feeling in those whom we teach; and the only method we have of doing this is to open, through countless ways, every possible avenue to thought, emotion, and expression and to keep ourselves alive while we are doing so."

Keeping ourselves alive in the classroom is both the challenge and the joy of teaching any subject. It is this failure—this calcification—that leads teachers no longer able to bend or see the humor of teenagers to misdiagnose what ails them as "these kids today."

In 1939, Mary Ellen Chase concluded her thoughts on teaching this way: "What we are after is an awakened consciousness, differing in each individual, an excitement in thinking, reading, and writing for their own sake, new discoveries, new enthusiasms, the casting off, or the retention with better understanding, of the old. What we want is to stimulate the love of mental adventure and constructive doubt, to create emotional satisfaction in the things of the mind, to reveal through books the variety and the wonder of human experience.

"How we do these things matters not at all. The numberless ways of their accomplishment reside in the numberless personalities of those of us who teach. The one thing that does matter is that we shall be awake and alive, alert and eager, flexible and unperturbed, likable and exciting."

Kids haven't changed since then, and neither have good teachers.

WORKS IN PROGRESS

February 9, 2002

IF YOU MISSED *Frontline's* recent "Inside the Teenage Brain" on PBS, you will have to wait another month to see it, and only then if you buy it. So many people have ordered the tape that it is currently backordered, an indication of the interest in the recent discoveries in the neuroscience described in the show.

Producer/director Sarah Spinks interviewed scientists, researchers, families, and their children to give an updated picture of what actually happens inside the brains of teenagers. What she discovered was both surprising and reassuring.

The biggest surprise is that human brains grow through two distinct growth spurts, one that begins in the womb and tapers off at 18 months, and the other beginning right before puberty and continuing throughout the teenage years and even into the early twenties.

Researchers have long known about the rapid development of infant brains, but the second stage of intense growth in teenagers is new information found during systematic imaging studies.

Scientists such as Jay Giedd at the National Institutes of Health have performed brain scans done in two-year intervals on children from infancy through adulthood and have traced the sudden change in brain development that happens immediately before puberty, when the brain goes through an intense overgrowth of cells and connections. At the onset of puberty, the brain begins the necessary pruning, or refining, of connections, eliminating the unused or weak ones and strengthening the efficient and strong connections.

Giedd argues that "use it or lose it" is the law of brain development. Whatever we spend our teenage years learning and practicing shapes the connections in our brains and establishes our baseline abilities for the rest of our lives.

Another great surprise about teenage brains is that they are organized somewhat differently from adult brains. Most noticeably, teenagers haven't yet developed the frontal cortex which is responsible for higher thinking skills and what scientists call "cognitive flexibility," or the ability to move gracefully from idea to idea and to reflect and plan effectively. Instead, teenagers rely on the more primitive, emotional, reactive part of the brain such as the amygdala to interpret data.

This was shown in a recent brain imaging study by Deborah Yurgelun-Todd, the director of neuropsychology and cognitive neuroimaging at the McLean Hospital in Belmont, Massachusetts. She showed adults and teenagers photographs of people's faces and asked them to identify the emotions the people were demonstrating. Adults in the study correctly identified the emotions 100 percent of the time. For example, when shown the face of a woman looking frightened, the adults correctly identified fear as her emotion. Teenagers, however, were not nearly so adept, missing the correct identification over half the time.

Yurgelin-Todd and her associates speculate that this inability to correctly identify the emotions of others may account for some of the classic miscommunication between teens and adults. Furthermore, the imaging studies implicate the emotion center of the brain as the reason for the misidentification—teenagers were using this part of the brain, rather than the rational, reasoning frontal cortex, to analyze the faces. If teenage brains interpret the world without the rational frontal cortex as a guide, that might explain the other baffling tendencies teenagers have for impulsive behavior and moodiness.

What does this new information tell adults who are struggling to understand and support the sometimes difficult teenagers in their lives? The researchers concluded that although teenagers look physically mature, adults need to remember that their brains are still "works in progress."

"It's sort of unfair to expect them to have adult levels of organizational skills or decision-making before their brains are finished being built, "Giedd argues.

Yet public policy is often based on that assumption. We allow teens with immature reasoning powers and a tendency for impulsive behavior to drive a car, for instance, and the trend in the justice system has been for stricter sentencing of very young juvenile offenders.

On the other hand, recognition of the important critical windows of brain development has already inspired some misguided public policy decisions, such as Gov. Zell Miller's hasty support of music CDs for each Georgia newborn, a theory of enrichment not supported by scientific research. Likewise, programs which promise to accelerate development are probably ineffective, too, since the brain seems to follow a definite pattern of maturation based on the age of the child.

Instead, adults can be most helpful by being patient and present, offering their own wisdom for guidance when teens flounder. Even teenagers seem to recognize this function of adults in their lives. Not too long ago one of my students slipped into my classroom before school began and asked if she could discuss a problem she was having with one of her friends. I was pleased but surprised, since this particular student is rather quiet, and our conversations have never been very personal in nature.

"I know I could ask my friends what to do," she said after she had explained her dilemma, "but they would just have kid solutions. I need a grown up to help me think about this."

I was happy to lend her my frontal cortex. It was the least I could do.

WILLPOWER

July 1, 1999

EVERY DECEMBER when I unbox the Christmas ornaments to put on our tree, I consider throwing away the beautiful hand-painted one given to me by a grateful parent.

Her son was a student in my junior English class several years ago. From the first week of school, he struggled to keep up, never doing homework and rarely finishing classwork. After he failed the second major test, I asked him why he was having trouble. "I guess I'm just lazy," he said.

But he seemed more spacey than lazy. In class he was often lost somewhere in a remote reverie and was startled when I called on him. His school records showed a history of failing and repeating grades, beginning in elementary school, yet he had never been diagnosed with a learning disability or other handicap. He was polite and affable, shrugging off my concern indifferently.

By mid-term I called his mother.

"He's always been lazy," his mother said, but she agreed to take him for a medical evaluation. That doctor referred her son to a therapist who diagnosed attention deficit disorder—ADD—and suggested a trial dose of Ritalin.

ADD and ADHD, attention deficit hyperactivity disorder, are recognized by the American Psychiatric Association, though they are contentiously argued phenomena in research circles and the general public. Complicating the issue is the lack of conclusive physiological evidence that ADD and ADHD have a neurological cause—though several researchers, including Judith Rappaport at the National Institutes of Mental Health, have shown that affected children tend to have a smaller than normal right prefrontal cortex, caudate nucleus, and globus pallidus in their brains. Not surprisingly, those areas control impulsiveness and distractibility in humans, behaviors which are hallmark signals of ADD and ADHD.

Still, diagnoses of ADD/ADHD are made not from elaborate imaging but from reported behavior, a much less objective assessment. Some physicians and researchers have even concluded that children labeled hyperactive are simply very active children with overly indulgent parents eager to medicate their children in lieu of genuine discipline.

Perhaps because the brain is the generator of our minds—our selves, our personalities—we often treat ADD/ADHD and other mental or neurobehavioral disorders as moral weaknesses or lapses of willpower instead of as physical disabilities. Illnesses such as schizophrenia, depression, and obsessive compulsive disorder were also once considered the tragic results of poor parenting, early trauma, or morbid stubbornness; they are now recognized as dysfunctions of specific areas of the brain and are treated with medications.

As the technology improves for actually seeing the brain at work and as the scientific understanding of the molecular level of the process of thinking evolves, we will treat the brain as we currently treat other organs. We don't judge diabetics who compensate for a defunct pancreas by taking insulin; we don't blame heart patients who are dependent on rhythm regulators. Neither should we demonize people who suffer from brain disorders which are able to be treated with medication.

Medication isn't the only treatment, of course. Behavior modification can be extremely useful in improving social skills, organizational techniques, and problem-solving strategies. Children with mental disorders are quickly ostracized by their playmates; consequently, they miss the interaction that helps them adapt and adjust to social situations. Their self-image is poor; their responses to being snubbed are maladaptive and defeating. The earlier the treatment, both behavioral and medical, the more likely the child is to have a normal childhood, and later, a healthier adulthood.

My student was 18—almost an adult—when he was finally diagnosed with ADD. He agreed to the trial dose of Ritalin, and by Thanksgiving he had become a star pupil. He came to class prepared; he read all his assignments on time; he turned in every paper. Instead of staring vacantly into the distance, he became an active participant in class discussions. His friends noticed the change and nick-named him Cinderella.

"All my life I've been walking around in a fog," he told me. "For the first time, I feel like I am the person I am supposed to be." That Christmas his mother sent me the ornament.

By Easter, he was failing tests again and coming to class unprepared. He had stopped taking the Ritalin after a popular news magazine and a TV talk show had brand-ed stimulant therapy as a poison and a crutch.

"If I try hard enough," he told me, "I know I can beat this."

But he couldn't, and he didn't.

Believing something doesn't make it so, regardless of the force of our belief. Toughing out a mental disorder is not a virtue, especially when effective treatments are available.

We would do better to encourage rigorous scientific research rather than publicly and stridently declare our opinions in the popular media where they can be misin-terpreted and misused. Someday we may have conclusive answers about the causes and treatments for ADD/ADHD and other disorders, but in the meantime, that Christmas ornament is a painful reminder of a bright young man who may never become the person he is supposed to be.

SLEEPING IN

February 23, 2002

WHENEVER MY SISTER DARLENE AND I reminisce about our teenage years, we eventually talk about the vacuum cleaner. Ancient, heavy, and loud as a tornado, it was my mother's weapon of choice to rouse us from our Saturday morning sleep-ins. She would bump the vacuum into our bedroom doors until we stumbled out of bed, or if that didn't work, she would fling open our doors and march inside, the vacuum rolling ahead of her like a tank.

According to new research into the sleep patterns of teenagers, my sister and I were doing what children the world over do when puberty strikes—trying to sleep more as a result of our changing biological clocks.

Sleep researchers aren't really sure why, but teenagers need more sleep than either children or adults, over nine hours daily. Not only do they need more sleep, but the time of day when they are able to sleep changes, too.

Possibly because their sensitivity to morning light changes to a sensitivity to evening light, teenagers generally have trouble falling asleep before 10 p.m. Instead of feeling sleepy at night, teenagers are awake and alert, often not going to bed until close to midnight. Unfortunately, their schedules usually require them to wake up the next morning long before they have had nine hours of sleep, and consequently, the majority of teenagers are sleep-deprived.

Sleep deprivation for anyone has serious consequences, but for teens the consequences are disastrous. Trying to eke out a few more minutes of sleep, many teenagers wake just in time to drive to school, a dangerous activity because they are rushing and their judgment is impaired.

Another serious consequence of sleep deprivation in teens is the negative effect on their education. Researcher Carlyle Smith, professor of psychology at Trent University in Ontario, has examined the need for sleep in retaining newly learned material. In repeated studies, Smith and his colleagues have demonstrated the effect of the different stages of sleep on cognitive and motor skills. Students who got adequate rest after learning a new skill were able to retain it, whereas students who did not get a good night's sleep did not progress and even regressed.

"When you're learning something that is cognitively very difficult and very new, and you do get a grasp of it, you can do nothing better than go to sleep," Smith concludes. "The special worry with teenagers is that they are learning a tremendous amount. They're still learning a lot of motor skills, fine motor skills, as well as learning all sorts of new cognitive procedural material."

Not only is sleep necessary for our brains to process newly learned material, but brains that are asleep in class are not getting the material to start with. Look inside any morning class in America and you are likely to see students who are so tired that they are struggling to stay awake or who have given up and are sleeping in their desks. This concern about the natural sleepiness of teens in the morning has led several school districts to experiment with school start times. In Minnesota, for example, one district pushed back their high school start time to 8:30 a.m., hoping to improve academic performance. Although the students did post modest improvements in standardized test scores and in grades, the dramatic improvement was in better attendance and lower drop out rates, leading the district to pronounce the program a success.

This kind of success has led Zoe Lofgren, a California Democrat, to author legislation pushing for later high school start times to better accommodate the innate sleep patterns of teenagers. Nicknamed the "Zzzz's to A's Act," the proposal, which in January was sent to the House Subcommittee on Education Reform, would give districts financial help to cover the operating and administrative costs of revising high school hours.

Until that or similar legislation passes, or until the public becomes convinced that teenagers really aren't being willful when they stay up and sleep in late, districts such as Charlotte-Mecklenburg will continue to ring the first bell for most high school students at 7:20am. In the meantime, researchers such as Mary Carskadon at Brown University advise teens to turn down their lights at night and avoid any stimulating activities such as surfing the Internet or watching TV. Although she doesn't advocate "sleep bingeing" where teens sleep until noon on the weekend, Carskadon does say that an extra hour or two of Saturday and Sunday sleep can help teens feel more alert and less moody.

Patience is always good in theory and difficult to practice with teenagers, but the research should help this generation of parents be a little more understanding of their sleepy teens. At least, I hope so. I hate to think that today's teens will be tomorrow's old geezers telling tales about their mothers' vacuum cleaners.

STRETCHING WINGS

July 17, 2004

DURING THE SUMMER OF 1985 I was in a race with a building contractor to see who would deliver first. Fortunately he won, finishing our house a few weeks before the arrival of my first son. My husband and I had been married for seven years, living comfortably in a small cedar plank house out in the middle of nowhere, but when the pregnancy test came back positive, we felt the undeniable call of the wild and started building a larger nest.

This summer I'm in another race, this time with a family of sparrows who regularly visit my backyard bird feeder. They are ordinary chipping sparrows, practically unnoticed until one day I saw them flittering back and forth from the feeder to a scruffy bird on the ground below. As one of the sparrows hopped close, the scruffy bird shrieked and did a little wing-waggling dance. The sparrow dropped seeds into his mouth and flew away for a few minutes, returning later and repeating the same scene again and again all afternoon.

I know a teenager when I see one. Teenagers of all species are demanding at times and a little ruffled and uncertain. That teenaged sparrow can fly—enough to get himself out of the nest—but he hasn't quite learned how to soar. He can feed himself—and he does peck around on the ground when his parents aren't looking—but he'd rather chirp for some free chow when he can get it.

My firstborn, now an 18-year-old high school graduate, is eager to leave the nest we frantically built for his arrival. He, too, has mastered locomotion—driving further and further distances and even flying alone to rather scary places such as Honduras while his dad and I have stayed behind and fretted, both proud and sick with worry. He can feed himself if he absolutely must, though he prefers announcing suddenly and loudly that he is starving for a home cooked meal, the kind only a mom can deliver.

The sparrows and I have this summer to make sure that our offspring are ready to face their adult worlds. I'm not sure yet who will launch first.

The sparrow parents are getting their bird ready by leaving him alone for longer periods, time he spends sitting on low-slung branches stretching first one wing and then another, flicking them up and down and arching his neck forward into the breeze like a figurehead on a ship.

My teenager is getting tired of the last-minute directives from his parents, unasked-for advice on everything from ingrown toenails to keeping his checkbook balanced.

He doesn't need to hear these things so much as we need to say them, the way we comforted ourselves more than we reassured our children every night when we tucked them into bed and turned on the nightlight of their childhoods. We sighed our relief that our children were safely in bed, away from the world that was both more wondrous and more frightening since we became parents.

Ever since that first child's arrival, my husband and I have braced ourselves for his leaving. Indeed, raising a child is a series of letting go more than anything else—at first letting go of our own self-absorption and later letting go of successive images of who our children become. Our sadness at losing our infants is mitigated by the joy they bring us as active toddlers, and we barely have time to put away all the breakables before they are school children and then adolescents, ready to fly away, leaving our own hearts broken with pain and joy.

Autumn is coming, and with it the attendant miseries of bird life—cold winds and rain, owls and snakes and hunger. Hopefully the teenager sparrow will be ready to face the winter and the promise of spring beyond it.

My own teenager, although he says that he is ready—even eager—to head off to college 700 miles and another climate away, surprises us occasionally.

Look at this. My husband and I are shopping and we stumble into a good white sale. For once we are clever enough to think ahead. We are almost giddy buying dorm bed sheets and towels, fingering the fabric and weighing the colors against what we know our son likes, and when we sit for a moment for a latte, we remark that we are, in fact, building another nest, this one distant and auxiliary, but a nest nonetheless.

When we return home, our firstborn is there to greet us.

"Look what we have!" I say, excited, handing him an armload of linens. I expect him to be excited, too, or at least interested, but the look on his face is unusual, unexpected, unreadable.

"I thought you'd like them," I pout, and he quickly assures me that he does.

"It's just, well, you startled me," he says. "I guess this means I really am leaving."

He looks up and I see a hint of uncertainty underneath his confidence. Then a thought flashes through his mind and he smiles.

"I've still got the summer," he says, stretching one wing and then another, sitting on a low-slung branch, waiting for the autumn wind.

CONVERSIONS

October 26, 2002

THE NEW TESTAMENT story which fascinated me most as a child was Paul's sudden blindness on the road to Damascus. My sense of justice was gratified that such a violent man could literally lose what was already symbolically clouded—his vision—but the end of the story was not as satisfying. When Paul's sight was restored and he renounced his evil ways, I lost interest. Where was the drama in that?

As I have grown older, Paul's persecution of the early church and his blindness have become the least interesting aspects of the story. Instead, what fascinates me now is Paul's subsequent history—his apparently genuine conversion from one way of thinking to a radical new way of being. The cynic in me has taken notice of too many other adults who have sworn similar conversions only to lapse later into the old diet, the reckless driving, the careless attention to relationships.

Despite my cynicism about the ability of adults to change, I am forever optimistic about the conversions of teenagers. Because their futures lie ahead of them relatively unencumbered, they seem less reluctant than adults to strike out in unexpected directions, and watching them feel their way down new, more rewarding paths is one of the chief pleasures of teaching high school.

Recently two students explained their conversions to me in detail.

Jodi's enlightenment began last summer when Sue Hilton, the senior guidance counselor at our high school, struck up a conversation with her about the upcoming school year. As Jodi recalls, Sue told her, "You can either come back for your senior year and goof off like you have in the past, or you can decide to set a goal and make A's and B's."

When her senior year started, Jodi decided to rise to Sue's challenge. At the first midterm she told me proudly that her A in my English III class was her first.

"Your first A in English?" I asked.

"My first A in anything," she said.

Later when she received her nine weeks report card— all A's and B's—I asked, only half-jokingly, "Why did it take you so long to grow up?"

Jodi leaned over my desk conspiratorially.

"I had an image to maintain," she said.

With a heavy academic load to make up for missed opportunities in the past and a GPA lower than she would like, Jodi's conversion has come too late for an easy ride down the rest of the road. Her determination, however, will keep her headed forward.

Danny is another student who has seen the light in the middle of a journey, though his conversion began this fall when he left for college. Last year he and I were friendly adversaries as he slacked his way through my Advanced Placement English class, and according to Danny, his attitude was, "I made a B? What's wrong with you!"

On his first day of biology in college, Danny looked around at the 300 other students and realized that the cozy days of high school hand-holding were over. He diligently came to every class, sat in the front row, took careful notes, studied them, and almost failed the first test, which measured not the facts presented in the class lectures but the students' ability to apply those facts to unique situations.

"In college," Danny confided to me the other day when he drove home for a weekend visit, "the professors don't teach you the information. You have to teach yourself."

To his credit, Danny has discovered how to do that. He goes to tutors and studies each night for his classes. For the first time in his career as a student, he writes down due dates for assignments and refuses to socialize on school nights. When the professors have extra help sessions, Danny is there. When he is confused, he seeks out graduate students who have already passed the classes. His grades and his pride in himself have risen steadily.

"Think what you could have done last year in my class if you had been the kind of student then that you are now," I told him.

"I know," Danny said ruefully. "I could have been the valedictorian."

In his nostalgic movie *Radio Days*, Woody Allen shows a mother only too aware of the "could have beens" in her own life.

She scolds her school-age son for wasting time listening to the radio, telling him, "Go outside and play, or go read a book. Too much radio isn't good for you."

"You and Dad listen to the radio," her son points out, but the mother is undeterred.

"That's different," she says. "Our lives are ruined already."

Maybe. Or maybe as adults we can take this lesson from the young people in our lives—that blinding lights can lead to revelations, and revelations can lead us in new, more fulfilling directions, no matter how old we are. And that, it turns out, is drama after all.

REDEMPTION

May 21, 2003

THIS IS A STORY about the redemptive power of love.

Like most love stories it starts off happily, arcs through some setbacks and sadness, and ends up as happily— almost—as it started.

At least I think it does. I can only imagine the beginning. I haven't seen the end.

Wes is the main character of this story. I don't know how many people have loved him—certainly a mother and father, and maybe grandparents and uncles and aunts and cousins loved him when he was very small. They might have been the best parents and relatives in the world, taking Wes to soccer practice and making sure he ate a hot breakfast every day before school. His grandfather might have taken him fishing when he wanted to give him some special attention. Wes might have had brothers and sisters who laughed with him and mugged with him in family photographs. He might have had friends who rang his bell and asked him to come out to play when they were in elementary school.

Or maybe he didn't. I don't know, and Wes has never told me. All I know is that when I met him, he was an angry, hard-to-love 17-year-old. When he wasn't scowling at me, he was trying to sleep in my English class. Intelligent and self-destructive, he rarely finished assignments or finished them half-heartedly. Twice he cut my class and served suspension days. Once he came to school with a black eye and gash across his knuckles. By the end of the first grading period he was teetering on failure.

"What's going on?" I asked him one day when he was the last to leave after the bell.

Wes made some dismissive sounds.

"Ah, I'm all right," he said, dodging my question. And then, perhaps to hush me up, he said, "I'll do better."

He did—a little—enough to barely pass my class, leaving it almost as anonymously as he had entered it.

I don't know what classes Wes had second semester, but some of them must have been near my classroom because we often passed each other in the halls. He never smiled, but he always made a point of looking up out of the crowd and telling me hello in his clipped, direct way. His face was not quite sad, but lonely somehow, too old for a teenager, the face of a mill worker who lives for cigarette breaks, or the face of a boy whose teacher could conjure up a fictional sad home life and feel guilty for not getting to know his reality when she had the chance.

And then I noticed Wes was quietly courting a girl. At first I saw them together occasionally, and then all the time. Often I saw Wes escort his girlfriend to her class at the end of the hall and heard him running back the other way to his own classroom just before the tardy bell. He still spoke to me whenever our eyes met, and he still seemed too sad for a teenager, but at least I knew he wasn't lonely at school.

It is a truth universally acknowledged that a troubled teenaged boy, especially one whose vision of his future is short-sighted at best, needs but resents adult guidance. What is not always recognized is how that same teenaged boy can turn a deaf ear to the pleadings of a worried mother or teacher but will start taking school seriously when his girlfriend suggests he should. Wes was no different. I stopped seeing his name on the absentee and suspension lists. This semester—Wes' last semester in high school—he made the honor roll for the first time in his life. When I saw him in the hall, I asked him about it.

"Yep, it surprised me, too," he said.

During the last week of school for the seniors, Wes finished his exams and stayed late several afternoons helping to paint the traditional senior mural. This same indifferent kid felt connected enough to the school he once skipped to leave his permanent mark on the wall. Or maybe he wanted to stay and help his girlfriend, who was also working on the mural.

It doesn't really matter. Usually our attitude determines our behavior, but sometimes it works the other way around; we change the way we act and are surprised later that our feelings have changed, too. A boy works smart and gets his name on the honor roll, and he starts to believe he might have a brain. He donates his time to a class project, and he realizes he is a part of the school.

He imitates maturity to please that girl who mothered him through the terrible transition from boyhood, and he discovers he has become a man.

WARNINGS

March 26, 2003

THE FIRST THING you notice about the Templeton letters is how modern they seem. They were written on lined paper that looks as if it came from a kid's notebook, faint blue and pink guide lines still visible, though the paper is light brown after 140 years.

My brother Tim and I stumbled across the letters in a university archive while doing genealogical research on my father's family. The Templetons had known our relatives and had served with them in the same company in the Civil War. While our distant ancestors have remained mute, the Templeton letters offer us a view into the world they all knew.

"I sit myself down to write to you," every letter begins, the quaint formality obviously learned at home or at school. Their first letters are dated July 1861 when they were in Columbia training with other enlisted men, and they are full of the excitement of being away from rural York County—away from home—for the first time. The adventure of war fills their farm boy letters.

"We are going to get us some Yankees," William Templeton writes to his sister, and his brother's high spirits are echoed in notes to their mother.

When they leave the meager comforts of camp and begin their stint in the Army of Northern Virginia, the Templetons hint at hardships. One letter recounts a forced march through the mountains and the misery of stomach cramps and diarrhea caused by green apples eaten on the way. In other letters they ask that their slave Theophilus be allowed to bring them supplies: blankets, winter coats, a patched pair of pants left behind in a dresser drawer, and mostly, more shoes.

Then they go to Second Manassas, Sharpsburg, Fredericksburg.

Their letters become more pleading, more homesick.

Chancellorsville, Gettysburg, Cold Harbor, Petersburg.

"I cannot tell you the things I have seen," William writes when his sister complains of his growing silence.

Spotsylvania, Deep Bottom, Appomattox.

"We want to come home," the brothers say again and again, but only one of them does.

Last week one of my juniors in my high school English class told me that he is graduating this May—a year early—so he can join the war in Iraq before it is over. When he spoke of his patriotism, his boredom with York County, his excitement about testing himself in battle as a Marine, I shivered as the Templeton brothers whispered all around us of their own pride of service, their own terrible knowledge of war, their own loss of innocence.

My student is too young, too idealistic to hear their warning.

I wish no teenager ever needed to again.

SOLDIERS

September 6, 2003

THEY ARE TALKING ABOUT GUNS, but I am busy with first-day-of-school stuff and don't pay them much attention. After all, growing up in a rural corner of York County, the boys in my homeroom often talk about guns and are routinely absent on the opening day of every hunting season. For three years now I have eavesdropped as the same group of boys discussed deer stands and turkey calls, and this first day of school is no different than any other.

Or so I think until I hand out their new schedules.

"Edward, why does your schedule have only first semester classes?" I ask, puzzled. "Are you going to go somewhere else next semester?"

"Eye wreck," Edward says, and for a moment I don't understand.

"They let you sign up already?" I ask, and Edward says that he went through basic training this summer.

In January he will be a Marine.

I know these senior homeroom students fairly well; they have been mine since they were sophomores. I know Edward even better because last year he was one of my junior English students.

He's smart and lazy, at least with school work. He reads well but would rather sleep in class. When he works hard, he makes A's. When he goofs off, he still passes—usually—that's how clever he is. Like many other boys who are indifferent about school, Edward has sometimes seemed rudderless, drifting through adolescence without a real sense of direction. For him, the Marines is a destination, a job, something to do after high school. He is giving up his graduation ceremony to join early, though he probably doesn't mind much.

The other boy with an abbreviated schedule is leaving in January for the Army. Edward looks like a tough, wiry terrier, but Daniel is dreamy and artistic. The Army seems like a patriotic, romantic adventure to him, and he is eager to finish school and get to what he imagines will be the exciting part of his life. When he pumps Edward for information about basic training, his voice betrays some nervousness which he covers quickly.

For an hour on that first day of school they sit side-by-side in homeroom and talk, two boys suddenly set apart from their peers by the adult decisions they have made. The students around them listen respectfully, attentively, but their paths have already started to diverge. Edward and Daniel will be in Iraq when their friends are at the Senior

Prom. They will be experts in weapons and fighting by the time their friends are taking final exams in June.

I watch them for a few minutes after I have finished all my first-day-of-school stuff, thinking about the story I heard this morning on NPR about more soldiers dying in Iraq and Afghanistan. I think about my nephew who flew a helicopter in the first Gulf War and whose one and only postcard to me read, "Hello! If you like heat and sand and no girls, this is a great place!" I remember a therapist friend who commented recently that he has started seeing returning soldiers with post-traumatic stress syndrome. Finally I turn around and write something on the board so that none of my students can see my eyes tearing up.

At lunchtime I tell some other teachers about Edward's and Daniel's schedules, and Robin is as distraught as I am.

"Not Daniel!" she says. "He's such a good artist. I have some of his artwork in my room!"

We try and we try, but we cannot see Edward and Daniel as the Army and the Marines do. To us they are young boys who haven't yet read *The Canterbury Tales* or *Macbeth*, who still have some math and chemistry and history and economics to learn.

By the end of the day I have thought of Edward and Daniel about a hundred times. I think of them when I meet new students and when I greet returning ones. I think of them when I make a mental note to check on a student who ran away last year when her stepfather beat her up. I think of them when I chat with the autistic student who drops by to see me every day. I think of them when I assign textbooks and when I hand out diagnostic tests, when I gather up my books and turn off the lights of my classroom, and when I drive home.

And I think about them when I turn on the car radio and hear about more soldiers killed, and I think about those soldiers, and how some of them are boys just like Edward and Daniel.

GRADUATION

May 24, 2001

I AM BOTH the least observant and the most forgetful person that I know, but when Jane Nance spoke I understood immediately what she meant.

"We always had Joanne between us before," she said. We were sitting alphabetically at a recent school awards ceremony, guests of the graduating seniors who invite the teachers they feel have made a significant difference in their lives. Jane and I and most of our high school colleagues are often invited by our seniors, whose recent experiences in our classrooms still resonate in their memories.

Joanne was often invited, too, a surprise because she taught second grade. Her students had had 10 years of education since they last sat in her class, yet no other teacher had ever touched them quite the same way as Mrs. Munn, and almost every year one of them would ask her to be a guest of honor.

142

McSpadden, Munn, Nance—but this year, Jane Nance and I sat beside each other and talked about Joanne.

I didn't know Joanne the way you know a friend. I didn't know her favorite color or how she voted in the last election. She undoubtably had special recipes or funny jokes or private sorrows she shared with people close to her, but she never shared them with me.

I knew Joanne from her students, her second graders who ten years later sat in my senior English class and talked fondly of their elementary days. They may have said that Mrs. Munn was their favorite teacher because she made school fun or because she could explain things well or because she hugged them often, but at 7 or 17 when you say these things, you really mean that someone is your favorite teacher because you know with absolute certainty that you matter to her.

Joanne's students felt loved and important, so much so that years later when they cast about in their minds for the person who had meant the most to them in school, they thought of her first.

This year Jane and I sat side by side and remembered the last time we had been separated by Joanne. Two or three years ago when we were seated before the awards program began, I commented that Joanne's hair looked different.

"It's a wig!" she said laughing, and my face colored when—forgetful and unobservant—I realized that Joanne's recent chemotherapy had robbed her of her own signature silver pageboy.

She must have sensed my embarrassment, for she laughed again and said, "I really hate wearing this. At home I don't usually, but I didn't want to frighten anyone tonight!"

We talked some more about her cancer and her treatment, and then the ceremony began and the students were called to the stage to receive their awards, small medallions looped on stingy ribbons. The superintendent looked apologetic as he slipped them tightly over ears and ponytails.

"Oh, no," Joanne whispered. "My wig will come off!"

In spite of our alarm, we both snickered at the thought, but then we started to worry again. Could she just ease out of the line at the last minute, she wondered? Would the student who invited her be upset? Row by row the students crossed the stage and had noose-tight ribbons pressed over their heads.

The last row of students were lining up beside the stage when I told Joanne, "I have an idea. Since I go before you, I'll tell the presenter to just hand your medal to you."

But as it turned out, the teachers were not receiving medals at all. Instead, the superintendent shook our hands and handed us decorative pins in tiny boxes. Joanne and I giggled with relief when we sat back down, pins in hand and hair unmussed.

I have no doubt that some senior sitting at this year's awards ceremony wanted to bring Joanne as his guest but had to be content with bringing her in his heart, for although Joanne began the school year in August, she died this past December.

Now this May someone will stand up at graduation and make the ridiculous comment that these seniors are finally heading out into the real world, as if the students have spent their lives in stasis or limbo, not fully alive or aware. It is a foolish comment, one that I despise, because it reinforces an adult forgetfulness of the power of childhood and the permanent impact of its miseries and joys on who we become. Joanne's students were not sitting in her classroom waiting for some distant future when they would enter a world more real than the one she showed them with stories and pictures, with math lessons and spelling words. They were living in the real world then, the real world of second graders who already are able to know with a kind of youthful wisdom that this person cares about me. This person is in my mind and heart, and I am in hers. This person is worth taking with me when I leave.

And so they have. And so they will.

THE LARGER WORLD

January 26, 2002

TWO YEARS AGO Robert Putnam, Malken Professor of Policy at Harvard University, published the results of twenty-five years of surveys about civic engagement in America. In *Bowling Alone*, Putnam concluded that Americans today are far less involved in the public life of their communities than were their parents and grandparents. They vote less, sign fewer petitions, are more distrustful of the government and their neighbors, and spend little time with family and friends.

Last week Robert Putnam released the results of his survey of civic engagement since the terror attacks of September 11. Like many people who have noted the spike in patriotic rhetoric and unity since the attacks, Putnam wondered if the changes in attitudes and behavior would be permanent.

This recent survey shows that many Americans have indeed changed their attitudes—most notably indicating greater trust and satisfaction with the government—but few have changed their actual behavior. That is, while we may say we are united as a country, we still shy away from such community-building activities as joining clubs, supporting the PTA, going to church, or inviting friends over for dinner.

The one group of Americans who do record a change in both attitude and behavior are young people. Older teenagers and young adults report a greater sense of responsibility towards their communities since September 11 and show a surge of volunteerism and political activism. For this group, Putnam speculates, September 11 may indeed be their Pearl Harbor, that defining moment in their lives when they are forced to reevaluate their priorities.

As a high school teacher, I am not surprised that this particular age group has been most deeply affected by the tragedies. No group obsesses more about their immediate future than teenagers poised to leave home. No group is so idealistic and so charmingly naive as young people unencumbered yet with mortgages, children, and careers. They are fearless and free to instigate change in a way older Americans are not, both in their own lives and in their communities.

Yet older Americans are sometimes guilty of trying to protect young people from the shock of life-changing events. In fact, after many students across the nation watched live TV coverage of the World Trade Center and Pentagon attacks, some parents petitioned their school districts to ban any news coverage in school. Their concern about their students' happiness and comfort is understand-able—it is often the same concern that motivates parents to challenge certain novels in English classes, for example—but shielding teenagers about the nature of the world they will soon inherit is misguided and dangerous.

Even in my own class I sometimes wrestle with my conflicting desires to both protect and educate my students. Recently, for example, my American literature class read an excerpt from Olaudah Equiano's account of his capture in 1756 in Africa and his subsequent experience with slavery. Because Steven Spielberg's *Amistad* captures visually an almost identical picture of the horrors of the Middle Passage, I showed about fifteen minutes of the film after we had read Equiano's text. One stalwart boy burst into tears. More than one student looked away. Do I think the students need to know about our history with slavery? Certainly. Did I do the right thing to show the film clip? I'm not sure.

With my own children I am also sometimes uncertain about how much truth they need to know, though my older son taught me years ago that he is resilient enough to turn a painful truth into action.

When he was five years old, he badgered me one December night to tell him the truth about Santa Claus. I thought he was too young to deal with the disappointment the truth would surely bring, so I skipped around his questions and redirected him when I could. Finally, however, he put his face close to mine and said, "Mama, I really need to know. Are you Santa Claus?"

He was so insistent, so sincere, that I could not lie to him. I confessed.

"Good," he said, his relief palpable. "Then you're the person I need to talk to about what I want for Christmas."

If I were sure that every teenager could be as crafty, I wouldn't agonize so much in the classroom. When I watched the unfolding trauma of September 11 with my seniors, for example, I wondered briefly if we should turn off the distressing TV images and try to carry on with the normally-scheduled lesson, but my students were adamant that they needed to know what was happening in the larger world that day, and I agreed.

If Robert Putnam is right, they will continue to want to know what is happening and will transform their shock into a lifelong civic commitment. Their increased connection to the world and to each other might just be the best memorial to September 11 that anyone could hope for.

SAVORING COOKIES

WFAE July 9, 2001

WHEN I WAS MUCH YOUNGER, TV's first reality show was hosted by Art Linkletter. In a series called *Kids Say the Darndest Things*, Art would coax seeming wisdom and accidental prophecies from small children. At the time I didn't know that the show was reality TV. I assumed the wisecracking kids were fakes, prompted by whispering parents or desperate producers just out of camera range, but now that I am a mother, I realize that children are often keenly aware of the difference between truth and appearance and don't mind pointing it out.

My younger son, for example, when he was still little enough to be riding a Flintstone-style push car in the driveway, grabbed my sister's hand during a family outing and fingered her white gold wedding band quizzically. Then he touched my brother-in-law's hand and pointed to his matching ring and said, "Uncle Val, why do you and

Aunt Darlene wear these handcuffs?" We all laughed hysterically, but a year later they were divorced, and my sister told me that she had been shocked that day to hear my son speaking the truth about the misery they thought they were hiding so well.

Shortly after that family outing, we were driving in Charlotte when my son asked us to stop so he could walk around in the grave garden.

"Walk in the what?" I asked, thinking he was remembering a recent visit to a public garden.

"I said, let's go see that grave garden," he repeated, and I swiveled around in my seat and saw him pointing through the car window to a large cemetery, its flowered headstones as cheery as a garden to his four-year-old eyes.

Clearly he recognized that it was a cemetery, but it didn't seem scary or haunted or sad or dreary to him at all, just a place to walk around and enjoy the scenery, a place people might want to come to relive happy times. Or, at least that's what cemeteries can be, after the blazing hurt and grief burn away into the embers of memories that keep us warm.

More recently, this same son crafted a metaphor so apt that it has become part of our family vocabulary. One Friday my husband and I were listing the chores and commitments we had scheduled for the weekend, and my exasperated son rolled his eyes and sighed.

"Don't you think you should do your chores?" my husband asked him, and our son replied to us with the patience of a gifted professor burdened with simpleton students.

"Yes, I know I have to do chores," he said, "but the weekend is like a cookie. When you say that I have to clean my room, that's like a bite out of the cookie. Fold the clothes. Bite. Weed the garden. Bite. Finish your social studies project. Big bite. Pretty soon all the cookie is gone and it's Monday and I have to go back to school."

He's right, of course. As adults we are too busy rushing through life to notice a sister's crumbling marriage, too harried to notice the beauty of flowers wherever we find them. We insist on gobbling our cookies instead of really tasting them, swallowing them whole, careening faster and faster through our days, our weeks, our lives.

But once in awhile, if we are very lucky, children remind us to look more carefully at what we assume to be true—and to stop and smell the cookies.

DIVERSITY

SIDE BY SIDE

THE SAME PEOPLE KEEP DYING.

Or at least it seems that way. Every day when I scan my small town's obituaries, the names are always the same. Wallace and Davis, Gladden and Cook. Each week a Bratton dies, and a Bailey, a Bennett, a Blackmon. People named Harris and Dunbar and Roberts and Robertson are laid to a peaceful repose with other descendants of the Scots-Irish and the English who settled this area centuries ago.

When the Declaration of Independence was read to the troops in the field, Charlotte was the frontier of the new United States, but the Scots-Irish were already here. My ancestor William Darwin from Louisa County, Virginia, joined them when his two-year tour of duty with George Washington was up, lured here by the stories of easy land terms and lots of elbow room. The house that his son built in 1800 still stands out in the middle of nowhere, but even

155

it is not as enduring as the surnames of the families who have continued to live near it.

Yet this clannish sensibility is beginning to change. Although I have spent most of my years teaching White-sides and Williamsons and Wilsons, I have begun to have students named Tovar and Ramirez, children of migrant workers who farm the local peach orchards.

Recently I taught Priya Patel, who moved from India when she was three, and last year I taught LaChanda Anaga'Nwoke, whose father is from Africa. When I saw her listed on my roll before school started, I asked one of her former teachers to give me a quick lesson on how to pronounce her name—which I did correctly the first time I called the roll, something that tickled and surprised her.

The year before that I met my first truly non-phonet-ic Polish name when Matthew Kalemkiewicz was my stu-dent. How in the world is *wicz* pronounced, I wondered, but too late. I had not had the foresight to get a pronun-ciation guide for Matthew, so I stumbled over his name the first time I called the roll, something that neither tickled nor surprised him. He sighed and his school buddy gave me this advice: "Just remember, Mrs. McSpadden. *Call-him-cabbage.*" Matthew nodded. It was close enough.

Since then I have met Resignos and Wangs and Tibliers and Nguyens and Zamoras, immigrants from every-where. I've seen young culture-shocked teenagers enter my high school speaking no English at all, becoming fluent by the time they graduate three years later. I've seen English textbooks become more inclusive of world literature—

even my American literature text—the most recent edition incorporating literature from Latin America, Canada, and Mexico as well as the more traditional literature from the United States.

This expansion of our circle from a tiny Scots-Irish enclave to a larger community is threatening to some people, their xenophobia more pronounced because the changes are new, perhaps, their letters to the editor hostile and full of complaints about what they perceive as encroachments on their traditions. For others, the influx of different cultures is rejuvenating, and the fusion of foods and arts helps smooth the way for a deeper appreciation of the Other.

Even the obituaries are changing—now the Boyds and Johnsons and Mac-Something-or-Others are interspersed with Espinozas and Cheungs.

Surely if we are destined to spend eternity side by side in the same Southern cemetery, we can learn to live comfortably side by side first.

PREP SCHOOL PURGATORY

April 24, 2004

THE STORY IS HORRIFIC—epic betrayals, theft, lifelong friendships broken. Hannah Friedman, a teenager from New York, wrote in *Newsweek* about her senior year at a private school this way: "The giggly familiarity that once pervaded the hallways of my prep school quickly morphed into a backstabbing mentality that consumed cheerleaders and calculus whizzes alike."

Her fellow students were so competitive and so obsessed with admission to college that they stole each other's required reading assignments. They spent thousands of dollars on SAT prep classes and weeklong summer camps designed to shape up their entrance essays. They broke into the guidance office and stole each other's records so that they could harass their competition for the same colleges. Best friends stopped speaking when one was accepted to college and the other was wait listed.

Is that what it takes to get into an Ivy League school these days? Private academies and tutors? A miserable last year of high school focused not on learning but on leaving?

Even Hannah reveals at the end of her column that she is relieved that she has been accepted to Yale and can now look forward to leaving the purgatory of prep school.

What a waste of a year.

Certainly many of the students heading off to Yale and the other Ivy League schools have spent their senior years the same way. If you believe in any advantages of a private school undergraduate degree, you may think their sacrifice is acceptable. Yale, for example, has the dubious—or prestigious—distinction of surpassing Harvard for the first time in over a decade as the most selective college, admitting only 9.9 percent of its applicants.

Getting to be one of those students can lead families to make drastic choices like the ones Hannah Friedman described in her *Newsweek* column, but no one has to. Of the current students at Yale, 57 percent are from public high schools, not prep, parochial, or private schools, and the rising freshmen class statistics are about the same. My older son, who has also been accepted to Yale as a member of the class of 2008, is one of the many students who give the lie to the prejudice against public education in America.

Jamie will graduate in about a month from a public high school in South Carolina, the state often last or near the bottom of any measure of achievement. He rode a school bus in elementary school, went to schools that were a hodgepodge of diverse neighborhoods, and is graduating from one of only two high schools in the community, both with almost 2500 students. Yet all those supposed disadvantages haven't stopped him or his classmates from exceptional achievements. They have excelled in International Baccalaureate and Advanced Placement classes and have benefited from teachers who were intelligent and articulate. They have given back to their school by serving on the student council and representing the school in the performing arts and sports. They have logged hundreds of hours of community service and have worked after school in menial jobs to help pay for their cars and clothes. They have not had time or money for prep schools or summer college-admissions camps.

Most of the college-bound students graduating with my son will use lottery money to stay in South Carolina and go to fine public universities. Some have won merit scholarships to private schools such as Duke or Davidson, and a few will go into debt to go to the Ivies.

For my family, that's part of the rub. My husband and I have saved for our child's education faithfully with monthly paycheck withdrawals and investments, and after 18 years of care we have accumulated enough money to pay for one semester at Yale or Duke, schools which offer programs my son can't get at the local public colleges.

Every financial aid officer I've asked tells me that colleges expect families to pay a quarter to a third of their gross income each year for one child's education. According to this formula, for the wealthy, Yale or Duke is an incredible bargain. For those of us in the middle class, that formula makes a private university education an incredible burden.

As my son and my own students weigh the pros and cons of various colleges before the May 1st deadline, I keep thinking about Hannah Friedman and her miserable senior year of high school. No matter where the current seniors choose to continue their education, every year of school is too valuable to dismiss as a mere prelude to something more important.

In many ways Jamie has had the best of all possible worlds—one last year of challenges and fun at his public high school, and a future made brighter by what he has learned there. Here's my thanks to all his teachers, from the kindergarten aide who made sure he washed his hands before snacks to the senior math teacher who insisted, demanded, that her class learn calculus in a single semester. You are worth more than you were paid—and more than I can ever repay.

LINGUA FRANCA

March 25, 2006

THIS IS what I told my students to do:

Write a paragraph so full of description that it bulges with imagery. Hold it in your palm and squeeze, letting the pictures run like juice through your fingers. Throw away the pit and the pulp—the conjunctions, the silly helping verbs, the articles standing like mute palace guards before the nouns—and stir your pencil through the nectar left behind.

Or at least that's what I meant to say two weeks ago when my creative writing class began our unit on poetry. Predictably, several students were adamant they didn't like poetry and couldn't write it.

That's when I told them to write descriptive paragraphs that we would trim into poems. Even the dissenters stopped grumbling and agreed to try, and soon everyone in the room was busy scribbling away.

Even Juana.

As I walked around the classroom and read over my students' shoulders, I nodded and occasionally made a suggestion or a comment.

Until I came to Juana. I glanced at her paper and scanned it for any words I knew.

"*Amigos*? Friends?" I asked. "Are you writing about a friend?"

Juana's smile was apologetic and she shrugged her shoulders.

I walked on down the aisle, once again failing to reach this student from Mexico.

Juana is beautiful and shy, a sophomore who likes to read Spanish novels and plays from our school library. When I realized at the beginning of the semester that Juana knows so little English, I told her to write in Spanish instead, hoping that at least she would feel less isolated while the rest of the class was busy working and confident that I could get a translation afterwards. However, like too many of her English-speaking peers, Juana writes her native language with errors in spelling and grammar that confuse online translation software. While the Spanish teachers at my school were able to parse out more of Juana's meaning, I was reluctant to impose on them often, and I soon stopped asking them for help. Instead, I consigned Juana to the wasteland of my inattention.

I'm not proud of that.

Every day my creative writing class wrote short journal entries and read them aloud, and each day Juana read her Spanish paragraphs and the class listened for words they knew.

"I heard *gusto*," someone might say.

"Did you say *muchachos*?" someone else might ask. Juana would look cautiously around and smile.

"Thank you, Juana," I would add, stupidly.

For two weeks now we have written poems. After our easy introductory descriptive poem, we have tackled other types—epitaphs and confessions and parodies and memory poems—and every time I have sat beside Juana for a minute and explained in the halting language of a simpleton what I wanted her to do.

One day—perhaps because her poem had a word that lured me like a glimmer of gold in a dark mine—I pulled up a chair beside Juana's desk and asked her to tell me about the first line.

She couldn't—though I grasped that she was writing about flowers and thorns and honey—which were all really metaphors about herself. When the bell rang I was exhausted and frustrated, but I sensed Juana's affinity for figurative language.

The next time the ESL teacher came to the high school, I asked him to look at the poems Juana had been writing in class and to help her translate them into English so that we could include them in our class's anthology. The poem Juana handed to me later that day was a window into the soul of a girl who is a keen observer of the people around her, a girl homesick and nostalgic in equal measure, a girl buoyed by the optimism of youth.

With minor editing from me, here is Juana Mendoza's poem, a testament to the power of poetry to reveal our hearts and minds to each other.

Three girls:
The first, intelligent and studious
And the second, daring and flirty.
Ummm....the third one, brave
And above all, the most scared.

When one had a problem,
We applauded her onward
We were three sisters for each other
Three pairs of pants
Three toys, three ways of thinking,
Three roads.

Girls who liked to get dirty in the dust
Dust that now we kick up while walking
Dust that one day will settle
In one place
And not fly away
Anymore.

Three sisters who had no worries
No sins, no bad thoughts
And no lies

We are three girls
Though I say we are one
Although we are older

Our hearts continue
Being those of children
So innocent
And above all,
Full of patience.

WANDA

September 2, 1999

SUNDAY MORNING may still be the most segregated hour in America, but on Monday morning American children wake up and go to our most integrated, diverse institution—public schools. While opponents in the recent Charlotte school litigation argue in the courts and in the media about the role of government in determining the degree of racial integration and diversity, two federal laws passed in the 1970's have been quietly and forcefully integrating another population—disabled students—into the public school system.

The Rehabilitation Act of 1973 guarantees that all individuals, regardless of their disabilities, will not be deprived of their civil rights. Section 504 specifically applies to the public schools, requiring reasonable accommodations for students who do not qualify for special education but who may have some impairment in their educational performance. An example is a student who fractures his arm; his teachers might allow him to take taped tests instead of written ones. For students with a medical diagnosis of ADD or ADHD (Attention Deficit Disorder or Attention Deficit Hyperactivity Disorder), accommodations might include preferential seating away from a distraction such as an open door or allowing more time to finish an assignment to compensate for an inability to focus efficiently.

The other law which has helped integrate disabled students is Public Law 94-142, amended several times since it was passed in 1975 and renamed Individuals With Disabilities Education Act (IDEA). It states that all children will receive a free, appropriate public education. "All children" includes children with physical, mental, emotional, or behavioral impairments which significantly impede their learning.

Parents who suspect that a child may have a learning handicap should first contact the child's teacher and guidance counselor. The counselor assembles an evaluation team to look at the child's past school performance, current functioning, and any standardized tests deemed necessary. If the team agrees that the child qualifies for help under IDEA, an Individualized Education Program (IEP) is written which identifies the services needed by the student and suggests strategies for helping him achieve academic success.

By some estimations, over 12 percent of public school children require some form of additional help, either with a 504 plan or through IDEA. That equals 5.8 million children with disabilities, children who 25 years ago might have been turned away by school districts reluctant to assume the expense or the trouble of special education.

Wanda was a student who would have been turned away. She had her first stroke when she was 7, and by the time I met her when she was 17, she had lost the use of the right side of her body. She was frequently absent, her sickle cell anemia leaving her exhausted after late-night transfusions in the emergency room.

When she was in school, Wanda struggled to keep up in my senior British literature class. Beowulf's courage didn't come close to her own. King Arthur must have seemed like a spoiled whiner to a young girl whose every day was full of pain, whose only goal was to graduate from high school.

Wanda's mortality was never in doubt, not from the first IEP meeting where her other teachers and I learned that she had already outlived the most optimistic guesses of her doctors. Some brain dysfunction from the strokes made learning new material especially difficult, but everyone on the IEP team agreed to tutor Wanda before and after school. Because she couldn't use her dominant hand, writing was slow; her teachers let her answer many test questions orally to the daily resource teacher. When her absences sometimes stretched into weeks, we reduced the amount of work needed for her to demonstrate mastery.

I don't remember if Wanda actually participated in the graduation ceremony—she may have been too ill—but I do know that no student I have taught since ever valued her diploma more.

Some taxpayers will argue that Wanda's story is the reason the federal government should stay out of public education. She cost the district money that could have gone to educate more capable students who would later become productive citizens working to refill the public coffers. Instead, within a year of graduation, Wanda died.

Do I think the extra time I spent with her, that all her teachers devoted to her, was worth the effort? Do I think the school district was right to divert funds into special education? Of course I do. Wanda wasn't a statistic or an abstraction to me. She was a young woman whose short life was made happier and more meaningful by the public schools.

On a wall in my classroom I have posted my school's mission statement that comes very close to echoing a recent editorial from the *Charlotte Observer*. It states that our job as a public school is "to provide an opportunity for all individuals to reach their highest potential."

That's both a noble sentiment and a daunting task. Without the mandate of the law, for some children it would still be just a dream.

TRACY

February 9, 2000

THE FIRST TIME I ever heard the word "diversity" used as a racial slur, the faculty at the high school where I teach was meeting with a group of parents and community representatives to discuss our vision for our school and our goals for our students. During a brainstorming session when a black parent advocated adding more multicultural courses to our curriculum, a white parent muttered, "Diversity!" and walked out.

Soon I heard it used negatively again, this time by a teacher scanning his class roll the day before a new school year.

"Half these kids failed last year," he wailed, "and the others are on the honor roll! This diversity makes teaching impossible!"

For him, diversity wasn't a reflection of racial balance or ethnic or religious presence—it was heterogeneous scheduling which doomed his slower students to failure and his brighter students to boredom.

Since then I've noticed that "diversity" is one of the most contentious words in education. In the recent school reassignment plan, for example, many parents have asked the Charlotte-Mecklenburg school board to strive for as much diversity in the student population as possible, citing studies which indicate the inadequate performance of schools which serve mostly poor or minority students. Other parents have asked whether diversity is merely a statistical way of hiding underachieving students by averaging their scores with their academically successful peers.

Ironically, diversity may become a moot point as the curriculum becomes more test-driven. Although ample research confirms what teachers have always known—that students learn best from each other in active communication such as class discussions and study groups—teachers who feel the pressures of accountability in the form of standardized and end-of-course tests are tempted to use more efficient, though ultimately less effective, teaching methods such as lecture or independent seat work. Sitting beside someone of another race or religion to listen to a lecture does not make a classroom diverse. Sitting with that same someone as a research partner does.

But is an education with people from vastly different backgrounds and experiences worth the inconvenience of traveling to a school out of the neighborhood? Does it actually prepare students for living in a diverse American society?

Does diversity matter?

Witness my public speaking class.

It is the third day with my new students, the day that I will start to love them.

We have spent the first two days introducing ourselves and learning about each other; one boy who has a reputation as an angry troublemaker lives in a foster home; a heavy girl hides her shame about her weight with a liveliness that is dimmed when she recounts her mother's recent death; a junior who eats two free meals at school tells us that she is overjoyed that her father has found work after a year of being unemployed; a self-contained special education student is trying to learn to balance a checkbook so she can live on her own; a brilliant sophomore hopes to beat her SAT score of 1560; a single mother with a one-year-old daughter admits that achieving her dream of becoming a teacher is harder now; a professional's son plans on going to law school and thinks public speaking might help him deal with his natural shyness.

On this third day the assignment is to entertain the class with a story, so some of the students retell fairy tales; others tell personal anecdotes; one tells a story he heard in church.

Then I call on Tracy.

She doesn't move; I catch her eye and call on her again. When she still doesn't get up, I remember that her special education teacher has said that Tracy is often withdrawn and unresponsive. Social interactions are on her list of critical skills to learn before she leaves high school, but knowing this doesn't help me figure out what I need to do right now.

Suddenly the student sitting next to Tracy hands her a piece of notebook paper.

"Here," she tells her. "Pretend you are reading your story."

Tracy slowly stands, holding the blank paper reverently, a magic talisman. As she begins to speak, she isn't mentally handicapped but funny and clever, quickly gaining confidence from her attentive audience, stumbling over her words in a rush of contagious enthusiasm. When she sits down, one boy turns in his desk and says to the class, "She did a good job, ya'll. Let's give her a round of applause," and they do. Tracy beams.

That's when I realize I love them.

These students live in different worlds, travel different paths, see different vistas, and maybe always will, but at this moment, in this class, they are not part of the tribal clans called Us and Them, but fellow human beings enriching each other with grace and compassion and heroism, learning from each other lessons far more important than anything I can ever teach them.

And that's why diversity matters.

LETTER FROM A PARENT

March 3, 2001

Dear Teacher,

I'm that parent you have wanted to meet, the one whose special-needs child adds another challenge to your day. My child may be physically or mentally or emotionally handicapped; he may be white or black or brown; he may speak English or Spanish or another language at home; he may be in elementary school or about to graduate from high school. None of those details matter as much as his yearning to be free from labels, to be a normal child, to be accepted by his peers and valued by his teachers. Underneath all his categories, he is a human being in pain.

His world has limits that the rest of us can ignore. From his wheelchair he watches his classmates climb the monkey bars, climb the steps, climb behind the wheel of the driver's ed car. If he is mentally handicapped or learn-

175

ing disabled, he watches his classmates ace their tests, finish their homework with seeming ease, plan for college. If he suffers from Obsessive Compulsive Disorder (OCD) or Attention Deficit Disorder (ADD) or depression, his day is a torment of anxiety and unfulfilled potential.

I know that your classroom has many other children, all needing your time and attention, and my child can task your patience and resources, but for all the times you greeted my child with genuine affection, I thank you. Every time you have gone out of your way to acknowledge his contributions to your class as meaningful and important, you helped him believe in his own worth as a person. When you hushed the bullies or encouraged other students to sit with my lonely child at lunch, you made his life more bearable.

As you have modeled kindness and acceptance of my child in your class, you have taught every child watching you to live a more compassionate life.

Your best gift has been to recognize my child's impairment without letting it impair your vision of him as a child who can learn. You've set high goals that encourage him to strive harder without tripping him up with unrealistic expectations that leave him discouraged, and you have been creative in your efforts to help him grow. The time you have spent planning his instruction has been bartered from your own family or recreation, yet you have continued to try new techniques and to seek suggestions from your colleagues. You may have gone home many days despairing of the pace of his progress, but you have returned the next morning willing to devote your energies again to helping him learn.

My child is a handful—no one knows that better than I do—but that hasn't kept you from reaching out to him, teacher to student, adult to child, one human being to another. For the short time that you have known him, you have reached him with your mind and with your heart, and long after he leaves your classroom, he will carry with him your healing touch.

Yet for all that you have done for my child and for his classmates, I thank you also for what you have done for me. Long ago, on the day of the devastating diagnosis, I buried a phantom child who would grow up healthy and whole and began to live with my real child who struggles in ways that most people cannot fully understand. As you have tried to understand him and have loved him for who he is rather than rejecting him for who he isn't, you have healed me, too, and reminded me that my child is beautiful, not only to a mother who loves him fiercely as her own, but to his teacher who does not have to love him, but who does.

You've given me the extraordinary hope that even if my child does not live a longer life or a healthier life, he will at least live a better life.

And that, it seems to me, is what all real teachers do.

SNAPSHOTS

April 1, 1999

APRIL IS THE CRUELEST MONTH, at least for students in South Carolina's public schools. April is Test Month, and students spend a considerable amount of time in April taking standardized tests, including national achievement tests, the South Carolina Exit Exam, and the SAT, all presumably to show what lessons they have learned.

Later when the test results are published, parents, teachers, school officials, and students themselves struggle to understand exactly what these tests show. Do schools with higher scores have smarter students, better principals, or more talented teachers? Are their populations comparable to the schools on the other side of town? On the other side of the state line?

In South Carolina, York County is divided into four unequal school districts, each representing a geographically distinct area. During PTL's glory days, Fort Mill was the district with the most revenues, but since Jim Bakker left town, Clover School District has been the richest by far, spending more than three times as much money per pupil—over $6000—as the other three districts, thanks to Duke Power and River Hills, a wealthy Lake Wylie community. Still, Fort Mill's standardized test scores are ahead of the rest of us, reflecting, perhaps, the years of earlier spending which attracted corporate managers from Charlotte who moved their families to Fort Mill to take advantage of a school system less vast than Charlotte-Mecklenburg's. The ten percent minority population and the constant influx of upper-middle class professionals working in Charlotte are cited as reasons for the high test scores. By contrast, Rock Hill School District is far larger and more diverse than Fort Mill, and the standardized test scores demonstrate that as well.

And then there is York, my district since I began teaching English at the high school in the fall of 1982. Many residents are rural blue collar workers, farmers, or small business people who spent the summer looking forward to the opening of the new Super Wal-Mart. Their incomes, and the opportunities money provides, are lower than the professional parents of Fort Mill and Rock Hill, but their commitment and concern for their children is just as genuine.

What do their children's standardized test scores measure? Indirectly, perhaps, they show access to money and experience. They reveal which students are living in stable homes and which are the unidentified homeless who move back and forth between parents and school districts. A test such as the SAT is a measure of which parents had money enough to take the children to see the monuments in Washington, DC, and which ones have never even been to Charlotte. The SAT shows who eats cold cereal for supper and stays up until 3 a.m. taking care of several cousins while an aunt works overtime. The SAT points at poverty and says, "Thou shalt not."

As teachers and administrators, we can't fix the poverty, the lack of cultural opportunities, the dysfunctional situations that challenge our students.

We can focus on creative, enthusiastic teaching which makes learning a positive experience instead of another hurdle to overcome.

We can advise our students on opportunities available to them and encourage them to take the most difficult classes we offer.

We can do better public relations with the community and communicate more with parents, explaining why we need bond referendums and proving our efficient spending of public monies.

We can try to keep the advantages of rural life—wideopen spaces, outdoor sports, extended family close by, neighbors who know us well—while admitting the unmistakable advantages of access to a large city such as Charlotte.

Recently I saw a fifth grade display of a class project that revealed for me what no SAT can ever adequately predict. The students had been instructed to paste three or four photographs from home on a large sheet of paper and to write short explanations of their selections. Some students mugged for the camera in Disney World, New York City, Boston, Jamaica. Those students had pictures of recreational outings with their parents and siblings; photographs of Halloween parties, Christmas excesses, birthday celebrations. They wrote about the richness of their middle-class lives, the richness of their horizons.

Other children had selected photographs of themselves with their mothers, women still so young that some were wearing high school graduation gowns or prom dresses.

"Here is my father," one student wrote. "I met him this summer."

These students had pictures which seemed to represent a desert of life—a blurred picture of a dog labeled, simply, "A dog I saw once down the road." A hesitant-looking baby being handed the baffling gift of a cheerleader's baton, someone's porch with a broken chair, a picture cut from a magazine with no connection to anything at all from a child who wrote, "We don't got a camera. Sorry."

I didn't need any standardized test to predict their success. No one needs a crystal ball to speculate on who will go to law school, who will stock the new Wal-Mart.

Those optimistic 10-year-olds become despairing 17-year-olds by the time I meet them in high school. Sometime in a few short years they learn something more permanent than English or math or science or music. They learn that society is still dealing with the paralyzing effects of poverty, ignorance, race, discrimination. It's a lesson they shouldn't have to learn.

MOMENTS OF REVELATION

WFAE April 23, 2004

IT'S THE LAST PERIOD OF THE DAY on the first day of school, and I am standing at the door of my high school classroom as my students warily make their way to the desks. Usually on the first day of school my new students enter the room talkative and excited, but ironically, these public speaking students are mute as they file in and jockey for seats in the back of the room.

One of the first to arrive is Myra, a student that I teach in Advanced Placement English, the honors class for seniors. In 25 years of teaching, I have rarely met a student with Myra's intellectual prowess, and she is a clear winner in the race for valedictorian of her class.

Seated behind Myra is a small black boy, probably a sophomore, who refuses to make eye contact with anyone. On the row across from him are two girls with pink and blue hair, their black clothes spangled with spiky studs.

Immediately in front of my desk sits a tiny girl who clearly has Down Syndrome. Her eyes look enormous behind her glasses, and she clutches a purple notebook to her chest. She waves briefly to a stocky boy she knows from her resource class. He doesn't acknowledge her but sits down behind her. Later I will discover that he has Asperger's Syndrome, a type of autism which makes communication difficult for him.

Just as the tardy bell rings, Jerry slides across the threshold and looks around for a seat. The rest of the students look at him intently as he saunters down the aisle, swinging his thick arms and clenching and unclenching his fists. When he sits in the desk he looks jammed in, almost uncomfortable. He crosses his arms and scowls at the students still staring at him. They quickly look away.

As I call the roll and hand out books that first day, I can't help but feel a sinking worry that this class isn't going to work. The students are too different. One Hispanic girl and another recent Chinese immigrant are uncertain in their English. A couple of students tell me frankly that they didn't sign up for public speaking and are unhappy about being here. Even the students who did sign up confess that they are terrified of getting up in front of the class to talk.

"Don't worry," I assure them. "Speaking in public is one of the things adults fear most, too. On all the lists of things that frighten people, more people say they are afraid of public speaking than of dying!"

The class does not find this comforting or amusing. I sigh and put the first assignment on the board, my students looking like alarmed deer. The first assignment is to write a 10 minute entry in a journal. I tell the students that they can write about the topic I suggest or about anything they prefer, but they must write for 10 minutes and they must be willing to read aloud to the class.

"The best vacation I ever took was...." I write on the board. When I turn back around only a few students have opened their notebooks and are writing.

"Get started," I prompt the others, pulling my stopwatch from my top desk drawer. Then I open my own notebook and write with them.

I glance up once or twice to judge their progress and meet the startled gazes of several students who are obviously stumped for anything to say. Tracy, the girl with Down Syndrome, is bent almost horizontal, her eyes only a few inches from her paper. She looks up to see if Myra is still writing—she is—so Tracy leans back into her paper and writes some more. Jerry is still scowling crossarmed, though I notice that his notebook is open.

Finally the timer goes off and I ask for volunteers. The students shift uncomfortably in their seats. Myra looks at me. Do you want me to start, she seems to ask with her glance. Yes, I telegraph back, and she says out loud, "I'll start."

Her writing is clever and chatty and totally engaging. It is also, unfortunately, totally intimidating, particularly for the sophomores in the class who seem to be in awe of Myra and the other seniors. I see one girl close her notebook when Myra finishes reading.

"Brittany, why don't you read yours next?" I say to her, but she says, "It's no good," and shakes her head.

This sort of mutiny can sabotage a class such as public speaking, so I needle Brittany a little bit until she finally opens her notebook back up and reads a very short account of a trip to Myrtle Beach.

"I told you it wasn't any good," she says. She doesn't seem to hear my reassurances that she's off to a good start.

The rest of the period is a fog of smoke and molasses. Everyone is relieved when the dismissal bell rings.

Fast forward to two weeks later on a Friday. The tardy bell rings and 25 students look up at the board where I have written, "One thing you need to know about me is..."

By now everyone has mastered the routine of writing in their journals at the beginning of the class, but so far the students have played it safe, rarely revealing much of themselves in what they write. Today, however, everyone begins writing immediately and writes fast and furiously.

I write with my students, too, but the atmosphere in the room is so electric that I keep looking up. Jerry is glaring intensely as he hunches over his journal, rivaling Myra in intensity. When the goth girls write, their heavy chain bracelets drag rhythmically across the desk top.

On the front row Tracy presses so hard that she breaks her pencil point and gets up to sharpen it. The boy with Asperger's writes a few sentences, pauses, rubs his hand through his hair, and writes some more.

When my timer beeps, Jerry waves his hand in the air to catch my attention and asks to read first, which surprises me since he usually doesn't want to read at all. Until today, he hasn't written more than two sentences for each journal entry.

As he begins to read, every student slowly turns to watch him. Jerry tells us that what we need to know about him is that when he was eight years old, his parents were arrested for selling drugs and spent several years in prison. Jerry has lived with so many foster families in the past 10 years that he has lost count of them all. The last family was so heavy-handed that Jerry got a job at night stocking the shelves of a grocery store so that he could afford the rent on his own apartment, a place that by his description is unbelievably bleak, a carpeted room without a TV or a phone. It is, however, his home.

When he stops reading, one girl says softly, "My dad's in jail, too."

In some mysterious way Jerry's journal entry and the class's response elevates us beyond the confines of the classroom. The next student's story is very different from Jerry's—a happy memory about something she has done with her family—but she reads with more sincerity and more honesty than she has before. So does the next student, and the next, until everyone has finished.

After a day like this, I know that our journals will stop being writing exercises and will become moments of revelation. I watch this miracle happen each spring when I teach public speaking. All it takes is for one brave student like Jerry to begin transforming a classroom of individuals into a community of empathetic, trusting equals.

ANGRY GIRL

August 29, 2002

THIS IS A STORY without a happy ending, at least not yet, and maybe not ever.

If this were a fairy tale, I would be the evil stepmother and the angry girl would be Cinderella, but it is a real English class and I am the teacher who is making the angry girl's life miserable by insisting that she work from bell to bell.

For the first week or two of school, some of her classmates were as vocal about the amount and difficulty of work required in English III. The angry girl could get a disruption going quickly by saying loudly to no one in particular, "Why is she making us do all this work? I never had to work this hard before. I'm just not going to do it."

"Yeah," her buddies would chime in, though in a few minutes they would be back to listening carefully to the stories I read aloud to them or puzzling through a worksheet with a partner. That is, everyone except the angry girl.

As the weeks have progressed, fewer students have joined her in her requisite grumbling and griping until now no one does, and, in fact, they often tell her to be quiet. Her classmates are attentive to my teaching, listening to the selections from the American literature book and taking notes from the board. The angry girl has her head down on her desk, though she continues to mumble adolescent jibes at the amount of work, my handwriting, the temperature in the room—anything to let me know that she is still awake and angry.

Her classmates are making top grades on their open notebook quizzes, but the angry girl has failed both major tests. Students far less capable than the angry girl are starting to show progress in their essay writing and in their ability to reason through the analytical worksheet questions. The angry girl has decided that she would rather try to talk to the people around her or badger the people in the room she doesn't like—especially me—and her poor classwork grades both reflect and fuel her anger.

I don't understand the depth of her anger. Though I have tried to be helpful and respectful to her, she has been unfailingly unkind to me and her classmates, skirting the edges of outright disrespect and antagonizing the students who try to befriend her. If she ever smiles, I haven't seen it.

Sometimes before class I try to understand her anger when I hear her talking to the other students who live in her neighborhood, their stories about relatives killed in drug deals, parents who have given up trying to corral their wayward children, and the constant illnesses that afflict the poor. They sometimes mention their dreams—usually about money, rarely about finding personal fulfillment.

"If I could find a job that paid about $100 a day," one boy said to the angry girl recently, "I'd quit school in a minute."

"I'd leave for a lot less," she replied.

In almost every class in every school is someone as shortsighted and as angry as the angry girl, yet most of those students find some inner strength or external motivation to help them muddle through. If this were a fairy tale and I had a crystal ball or a magic mirror, I could see which students will be able to muster the necessary resources to be successful and which ones, like the angry girl, are more likely to fail.

But this is the real world, and I don't know why some students from horrible backgrounds and with overwhelming odds against them prevail and why others crumble. If I did, then I might be less at a loss for what to do for the angry girls and boys that come into my classroom.

That's why I'm very glad that the South Carolina Department of Education is hosting a series of meetings called "Closing the Achievement Gap." Mental health professionals and community leaders are being invited to join educators to discuss strategies for helping low-income students and to explore the connection between physical health and academic achievement, among other topics. The emphasis is on the achievement gap between white and black students, but all students should benefit from an increased understanding of the role that communities and parents play in their children's success in school.

Their findings and recommendations will probably come too late for the angry girl. She and I have our own private gap that I haven't been able to bridge—at least not yet, and maybe not ever.

Still, I couldn't be a teacher if I didn't believe in at least the possibility of a happy ending.

OUTCASTS

January 31, 2004

SHE ALMOST dropped out in October.

She should have been in my Advanced Placement English class, a fifth year of English for students identified in junior high as talented in language. Instead, as a senior she is in a regular college prep English IV class, a year behind expectations after missing so much school last year.

She will tell anyone who asks that she is to blame for missing so many days. She doesn't blame her absent mother, her abusive ex-boyfriend, the neighborhood gang, or the lure of easy money selling drugs.

She doesn't blame her poverty, her race, her experiences in school, or the culture of pressure from her peers not to succeed.

She could, but she doesn't.

In my CP IV class she is quick to see connections and is outspoken in her interpretations, holding her own in heated debates and often staying behind a few minutes after the dismissal bell to ask an extra question or two. Her insights into literature and human nature are a blend of her innate ability and her early walk on the wild side.

She would have been a great student in Advanced Placement English.

That she isn't is a measure of the achievement gap that bedevils American schools all across the country. Numerous studies document the disparity between the standardized test scores, grades, and graduation rates of Asian, white, black, and Hispanic students. Asians and white students as a whole outscore black and Hispanic students, who are more likely to be poor.

The explanations for the persistent achievement gap are well known and widely discussed. Most researchers name poverty as the most significant hindrance to student learning. Families living in poverty are more likely to have premature or underweight babies, suffer more hunger or food insecurity, have less time or money for quality pre-school activities, and rely on TV as entertainment rather than books or trips to museums and libraries. Children from poor families begin kindergarten already scoring below average in general knowledge and reading readiness. Most of them never catch up.

Factors within the school system can also keep students from achieving their full potential. Inner-city and rural schools are often underfunded and have less extensive curriculum offerings than wealthier suburban schools. Teachers in those systems make less money and have less experience and education on the whole than teachers in more affluent systems. Students in poor school districts may have fewer materials and reduced expectations of their performance.

Any one of those external factors can negatively impact a particular student's ability to learn in school. My student who almost dropped out, for example, might not have gotten off track if she had not had to deal with such a constellation of problems, though she is adamant that she could have overcome them if she herself hadn't made foolish choices.

John McWhorter would agree. In his controversial book *Losing the Race: Self-Sabotage in Black America*, the Berkeley linguist argues that despite all of the external factors impacting student achievement, the internalized ideas of modern black culture are also part of the explanation of the achievement gap. Young black students in America, McWhorter claims, have been taught to see themselves as victims and to distrust education as a white activity. Doing well in school brings ridicule from other black students and threatens to make high achievers outcasts from their peers, something McWhorter says he experienced even in an upper-middle-class neighborhood and school.

I've certainly seen this kind of harassment in school, and I've heard many of my African American students complain that their friends accuse them of somehow betraying their racial heritage by taking honors classes and making top grades. For many students, the loss of their peers is too high a price to pay. Others, like my student who almost dropped out, turn themselves around from the brink and take pride in their strength of character.

Although some in the black community take issue with McWhorter's claims of a pervasive black culture, others, such as *Chicago Tribune* columnist Clarence Page, have recently written about their growing convictions that parental expectations and social pressures have as much to do with student achievement as anything that happens inside the schools.

What happens inside the schools as well as what happens in society as a whole has to be examined if we are going to make any real progress on closing the achievement gap. Not many students can overcome hurdles so high that leaving school seems like the only solution—nor should they have to.

ROLE MODELS

August 27, 2005

THIS WAS SUPPOSED to be his senior year in high school, and he was supposed to be sitting in my honors English class.

Instead, he is sitting in prison, serving a five-year sentence for selling drugs.

His classmates will be finishing college when he gets out. They will be heading to graduate school or starting their careers about the time he realizes that no one will hire him.

We've probably lost him.

And we're losing a generation like him, African American boys leading the country in rates of homicide, suicide, HIV/AIDS infection, unemployment, incarceration.

Social scientists can point to multiple factors that impact black males negatively. Dr. Pedro Noguera, a professor at Harvard's Graduate School of Education, divides the scientific researchers into two camps, the structuralists and the culturalists. The structuralists implicate the environment, suggesting that economic forces—the availability of jobs, for instance—determine how individuals act. Structuralists argue that crime, drug abuse, and dropout rates are the results of social and economic inequality.

On the other hand, culturalists believe that individuals make choices based on the values, norms, and beliefs of their culture. They argue that solutions aimed at social equality—such as increased funding for schools—do not address the issues of personal responsibility.

Noguera suggests that both sides have a point.

"Both structural and cultural forces influence choices and actions, but neither has the power to act as the sole determinant of behavior. Even as we recognize that individuals make choices that influence the character of their lives, we must also recognize that the range of choices available are profoundly constrained and shaped by external forces," Noguera writes in the May 2002 issue of *In Motion Magazine*.

"Black males may engage in behaviors that contribute to their underachievement and marginality, but they are also more likely to be channeled into marginal roles and to be discouraged from challenging themselves by adults who are supposed to help them."

As the adults charged with helping children, teachers are particularly concerned about the educational achievement gap between black boys and all other groups of students. When standardized test scores are disaggregated, black boys score lower than their peers. They are over represented in special education classes and underrepresented in the honors classes.

Certainly structural problems such as poverty are hampering young black men, though middle-class black boys are also scoring near the bottom of the heap. In addition, black girls growing up in poverty outscore the boys, suggesting that gender differences have a hand in how boys learn—and are taught—in school. Young white boys growing up in poverty also outscore black boys, pointing to race as another important consideration.

Most intriguing of all, the achievement gap is evident all across the United States, regardless of location or type of school—and it is true in the United Kingdom, as well. Diane Abbott, a Labour MP, says that one way to close the gap is to provide more elementary school black and male teachers to serve as models and mentors. Educators in this country agree.

Stanford University professor Nell Noddings writes, "Young black men and boys growing up without male role models and in conditions of poverty probably do need, more than anyone else, that assurance that someone really cares. Many studies show the single most important thing in turning lives around is the ongoing presence of a caring adult."

This past Monday I listened as Cedric Jennings spoke about the importance of the caring adults in his life. When he was a junior in a chaotic inner-city high school in Washington, DC, Jennings became the subject of an article by *Wall Street Journal* writer Ron Suskind. Suskind wanted to write about African American students who were successful despite the environmental and cultural pressures facing them, but he had trouble getting any students to talk to him. The honors students were "undercover," unwilling to risk becoming the target of ridicule. Only Cedric Jennings seemed to have a "hope in the unseen," a belief in possibility that ultimately led to his getting accepted to Brown University. In his talk at the York County Public Library, Jennings mentioned some of the hardships of his life—poverty, a single mother, a father in prison, hostile classmates. Yet he was also uplifted by the unfailing support of his mother, and many ministers, community members, and teachers made him feel worthy and capable.

"I'm thankful for all of the people who encouraged me," Jennings said, "and even for all the people who tried to discourage me, because they made me stronger."

Not many young people are that resilient. Indeed, the persistence of the achievement gap suggests that African American boys are particularly vulnerable. Our task is to find a way for them to become successful anyway.

Some schools are doing just that. Schools that have a focus, which offer a challenging core curriculum, which couple high expectations with intensive support, and which are staffed with caring teachers are sending students into the world with a far better future than the one facing my student in prison.

SELLING STRATEGIES

August 12, 2006

I HAVE NEVER been able to sell anything, but when I was a kid, I was often forced to try. I was supposed to raise money for school clubs, for the student council retreat, for Girl Scouts.

"You don't want to buy any of this stuff, do you?" I would ask disinterested neighbors, and my low expectations were exceeded only by my lower sales. Usually I ended up having to buy the awful goods myself just to meet a quota—chalky chocolate bars, Christmas paper thin enough to see through, plastic flashlights with bulbs that dimmed and burned out within an hour of purchase.

How ironic, then, that I have spent my life as a teacher, a job which requires heavy-duty salesmanship.

Teachers sell every day. Before they tell their students to open their textbooks, teachers have to sell them on the idea that school is worth their time and attention. Before they can ask for help dealing with a child in trouble, they have to sell the parents on the idea that they are partners, not adversaries. When they talk with community members, they sell their perception of the public schools as places where children find success—or where they don't.

Students in high performing schools are easier to sell education to. Mostly from middle class and wealthy families, the students live with adults who are educated and have the resources of money and time to invest in their children. Their teachers look like them, go to church with them, speak their language, and understand their culture.

Students in lower performing schools inhabit a different world. Mostly minority or children of poverty, they may have families who want their children to succeed in school but have neither the resources nor the experienced savvy to help them do so. When they fall behind their more affluent peers in their elementary years, they disregard school as being relevant to them.

Teachers know this, which is why they resist being lured or coerced into lower performing schools. Teaching any student is hard work—you have to know your subject well and be nimble in selling it. But teachers in high poverty schools have to be relentless. We have to be uncompromising salesmen and tireless cheerleaders, willing to look squarely at the issues of race and gender and class that can sabotage our relationships with students.

High poverty schools can be high achieving schools— I've seen them—but they take more than charismatic principals and talented teachers. They need more than community support and district muscle. High poverty schools which have been successful in closing the achievement gap between whites and minorities, between girls and boys, all have one thing in common: They are able to get students to buy into a school culture that transcends any excuses or stumbling blocks that may have kept them from being successful in the past. They sell not only education but hope in a better future—and an insistence that the school has the best plan for getting students there.

This week I had to brush up on my rusty selling strategies as my new school year began. My school district, tucked away in the western corner of York County, South Carolina, shares many of the challenges that make selling education to students difficult. In York 61 percent of the students are classified as being children of poverty.

They all go to the same overcrowded high school. The ones who live in the most remote, rural part of the district get on the school bus at 6 a.m. They come from farming families, from families who were laid off when the mills closed, from the doctors and lawyers and preachers who have made practicing in a small town their calling. Some families speak no English at home.

Some children hear gunfire in their neighborhoods. Some children have never been to Charlotte, a city they can see dimly in the distance.

But none of that is on my mind when I walk into my classroom the first day of each school year and meet my new students. I am too busy shaking off those ghosts of my early selling failure.

"You don't want to buy any of this stuff, do you?"

Instead, I give a little spiel that also happens to come genuinely from my heart—which might explain why I wasn't able to move that candy and wrapping paper long ago.

"This class is hard," I say, "but you can do it. Even if you've never been successful in an English class before, you can be successful in here. I know lots of ways to help you be very good students in this class, but you have to do everything I tell you."

Then, if I'm lucky, enough kids buy what I say and pitch in to help me sell the class to their reluctant peers.

And thank goodness, too, because I need all the help I can get.

VISIONS OF THE FUTURE

November 20, 2004

"YOU CAN LEAD a horse to water, but you can't make him drink."

Or how about this: "If you build it, he will come."

These two cliches summarize my life as a high school teacher this month.

At my school a small group of students who took the South Carolina exit exam last spring failed it. Like many state exit exams, South Carolina's purports to test students' proficiency in three areas—reading, writing, and math. Students first take the exam their sophomore year, and if they fail any of the three sections, they retake the test again their junior year.

Failure in the junior year means that students have two more chances in the fall and spring of their senior year, but if they don't pass all three portions of the exam by graduation time, they do not receive a South Carolina diploma, even if they have successfully completed all their required courses.

Students fail the exit exam for a variety of reasons. Most are poor or suffer from learning disabilities. Many of them don't have the basic skills necessary to prove proficiency. Some don't have the maturity as sophomores to take the test seriously, or they are confused by the test format. Others don't have the foresight to understand the consequences of leaving school without a diploma.

As a teacher, I can't overcome my students' handicaps of poverty or years of falling behind in their skills—at least not quickly or completely—but I can familiarize them with the format of the test and suggest several reading and vocabulary strategies.

With that in mind, the English department decided to offer a crash tutorial for the juniors and seniors who were facing the exit exam this fall. Teachers told their students that they would be available for test tutoring before and after school.

The guidance counselors also identified all of the students who, because of block semester scheduling, were not in an English class and called those students in for a conference, impressing upon them the importance of doing their best on the exam and signing them up for tutorials. When the counselors handed me the names of a dozen students without an English teacher, I made individual lesson plans for each one, copying worksheets and sample questions in each student's area of weakness. Every morning and afternoon for two weeks we announced the time and place for extra help. Every morning the English teachers got to school early and left late.

And not one student showed up. Not one.

So much water and no thirsty horses.

But high school teachers are nothing if not optimists, so soon I was busy getting ready for my new group of SAT Prep students. One of the math teachers and I share the class, splitting our students into two groups and working for nine weeks with each one. This is the first year I have taught this course, and for this second group of students I had finally begun to find my footing and was eager to try a few techniques illustrated in some new materials. As the stack of practice materials grew on my desk and the practice questions remained on my board for a day or two at a time, my other classes of English students began to notice and ask about them.

"I need 30 more points on my SAT to get into Clemson," Mac told me one afternoon after our English IV class, "and I have trouble with the reading comprehension questions. Can I come in the mornings for help until I retake the test?"

"Sure," I agreed, and then I thought to ask, "When are you taking the test?"

"January," Mac said, and I inwardly shrugged. Good intentions didn't always translate into real actions. He wouldn't show up.

But he did—not just the next morning, but almost every morning since. And then another senior asked if he could come, too, and then a third asked if he could come during my planning period, all of them trying to tweak their SAT scores enough to gain entry into particular colleges. These students have the advantages of talent and motivation and a history of success in school that have given them what the exit exam students lack—a vision of themselves in a future of their own making, a future I failed to help my exit exam students see.

I don't mind all the extra tutoring or the hectic mornings blitzing through several SAT lessons with students this driven. If I build it, maybe they will come—and then they can leave better equipped to build their own field of dreams.

SUCCESS IS IN REACH

October 22, 2005

THE FOUNDERS of one of the most successful middle schools in America were two of this year's recipients of the University of North Carolina at Chapel Hill General Alumni Association's Distinguished Young Alumni Awards. Dacia Toll and Doug McCurry, Morehead Scholars who graduated in 1994, opened Amistad Academy, a public charter school in New Haven, Connecticut, six years ago. They wanted to see if a school tailored to the needs of disadvantaged urban children could close the achievement gap.

It can and it does.

In August 2004 the school was a subject of a PBS documentary which illustrates Amistad's success. Amistad is a school that is 97 percent African-American and Latino, 84 percent who qualify for free lunch. Most students enter the fifth grade scoring an average of two years below grade level, yet by the end of their eighth grade year, they are not only scoring as well as the wealthiest suburban students, in some cases they are even surpassing them.

On my last trip to New Haven I asked to visit the school and was graciously given a tour by Pat Sweet, the Director of External Relations at Achievement First, the nonprofit organization established by Toll and McCurry to replicate Amistad's success by opening other charter schools in Connecticut and New York. Sweet's background in community development and banking makes her an ideal choice to head the fundraising necessary to make up the difference between what the state gives charter schools and their operating costs.

Private businesses and philanthropists helped in the initial fundraising needed to convert a warehouse in a blighted neighborhood into an attractive school. Hanging over the entrance is a huge banner spelling out the acronym, REACH, summarizing the goals for students.

R is for RESPECT. Students at Amistad pledge to show respect for their teachers and for each other. This translates into observable behaviors such as raising their hands before speaking in class and keeping the building clean. On the day that I visited, I watched several incidents where teachers were swift to remind students of what constituted respectful behavior. In one fifth grade reading class, the teacher actually turned a student's head so that he was facing the girl who was answering a question. "Remember to look at people when they are speaking," she prompted.

E is for ENTHUSIASM. If any of the students were bored the day I visited, I didn't see them. I observed numerous reading, math, and writing classes, and hands were always waving in the air and small groups were buzzing with energy. Students who had met their REACH goals were proudly wearing their royal blue polo shirts. Students still missing the mark were wearing plain white T-shirts. Because the uniforms were a reward, they were "cool."

A is for ACHIEVEMENT. The mission statement of Amistad leaves no doubt that student achievement is their raison d'être. The curriculum is tightly benchmarked to follow state standards, teachers assessing their students each six weeks and using the results to plan instruction. Freed from the normal paperwork and discipline decisions by support staff, the principal serves as the real instructional head of the school, observing—and teaching—classes regularly and meeting with parents and teachers when students have difficulties. Students hear from their first day at Amistad that their goal is to graduate from college—and that all the hard work now will pay off in a brighter future.

C is for CITIZENSHIP. Student achievement isn't possible if students don't understand or buy into school culture. Students at Amistad are taught how to be responsible individuals in a community of scholars—and their allegiance to the procedures of the school shows. I saw one fifth grade class lining up by rows in the hall to go to morning break in the cafeteria. Two rows had filed out when the teacher abruptly called them back to the classroom.

"We have to start over," he said, "because someone was talking in the hall. Alex, you know how your mother has a radio at home with a volume button on it? You are going to turn your volume button all the way off. Now, let's try that again."

H is for HARD WORK. Closing the achievement gap takes hard work on the part of teachers, students, and parents. The school day is long—the 250 students arrive at 7:30 a.m. for breakfast and leave at 5:00 p.m., except for Fridays when they leave at 1:00. Mornings are spent focused on reading, writing, and math. Students learn social studies and science in the early afternoon and attend enrichment programs in computer science, art, music, sports, and other activities for the last hour of the day.

Can a successful urban school in Connecticut be a model for genuine school reform here?

UNC grad Dacia Toll is quick to say that no one aspect of the program is the key to the success of students at Amistad, that the talented teachers are just as critical as the consistency in lesson plans and school procedures, that giving students a belief in themselves and the tools to measure their achievements is as important as getting parents involved in overseeing homework. But Amistad's formula is clearly working, and those of us concerned about the achievement gap have everything to gain by learning what they have to teach.

LITERATURE

LET YOURSELF BE LURED

November 30, 2002

"I LIKE YOU BECAUSE YOU FIGHT BACK," Mike Stacey once told me. He was my principal at the time, and he wasn't lying—Mike loved a good fight. He argued everything with the same tilt and passion that he brought to his leadership, a style that afflicted the comfortable more often than not.

When Mike decided to go into education, the legal profession lost a potential courtroom marvel. In another age Mike would have had himself crowned Caesar. He gleefully butted heads with anyone who didn't have the sense to capitulate early—and I remember losing more than my fair share of arguments with him.

But one argument that I didn't lose came to mind when I opened my mail at school and found a new textbook sent out for advance approval. It is just the kind of English textbook Mike would once have applauded—heavy on practical exercises and lean on literature. In fact, the entire book is a collection of chapters on resume and memo writing, interview preparation, and other issues faced by people in the work force. The 30 poems, short stories, and essays are tacked onto the chapters as an after-thought, and the book is marketed as a "hands-on" tech prep book designed for students who will go straight into jobs or who will attend a vocational school or apprentice-ship program after high school.

To be fair, the "applied communications" approach to teaching English is a sincere effort to reach those students who are having trouble being successful in school.

According to the research, most successful students are those who are visual or auditory learners—that is, they learn and remember things they see and hear. Students who need to physically move around or manipulate tools in order to learn or remember have fewer opportunities to be successful in traditional school settings. Rather than make those students sit for long stretches listening to lectures or reading difficult materials, the tech prep approach encour-ages teachers to let them work in groups or demonstrate mastery of the material through projects and portfolios.

Where the tech prep theorists have gone terribly wrong—and where the textbook companies have followed their lead foolishly—is in underestimating the power of good literature to enrich every student's life.

Not everyone believes in the power of literature—at least not for teenagers. Mike didn't. Why should a weak student have to read an essay by Emerson, Mike asked, or struggle through a Shakespearean tragedy? Why does anyone have to read poetry at all, he asked, and this is what I told him.

Because through literature, we are connected to the rest of humanity. We hear from our ancestors and read the thoughts of our contemporaries. We learn how people in far places think about the world, and we see ourselves through their eyes.

Through literature we learn to think critically, to question those voices from the past and the present, to examine the concerns of those living far away and up close.

Through literature we learn who we are. What teenager, gifted student or not, isn't more interested in the universal concerns of literature than the minutiae of a good memo? Why is a class discussion about the dangers of Romeo and Juliet's impulsive behavior—and our own—not as valuable as a lesson on dressing for a job interview?

And why should the canon of great literature be a mystery to a student headed to the factory floor? Is the ability to read and understand a piece of difficult literature a skill only for the elite?

I told Mike that a good English teacher's job is to make the literature accessible to all students—using whatever teaching strategies work best.

"If you have never had a teacher who helped you feel that a piece of literature was relevant to your own life— that it spoke to you personally—then you have never had a good English teacher," I told him.

Mike agreed that he hadn't. Strict teachers, yes, and hard teachers, but none who gave him what he discovered later on his own, a genuine love of reading and a drive to be a lifelong learner.

For now I'll put that new textbook on a shelf and tell my junior applied communications students to open up their five pound literature books to a story or a poem or a novel chapter that can show them more than the world of work. Look here at yourselves, I will say, holding up a poem as a mirror of their experience. Let yourselves be lured, I will say, dangling a story before their eyes like a silver fish hook.

BORROWED EYES

June 3, 1999

ONE OF MY FAVORITE PHOTOGRAPHS is of my first son, then less than two years old, pointing to the sky with such excitement that he has raised himself on tiptoes, the object of his ecstasy an afternoon moon. Until my son noticed the moon, it was an unremarkable rock in the sky to me. Once he discovered it, I remembered what I had known and had forgotten since my own childhood, that the moon is both lovely and evocative, lonely and companionable, infinitely mesmerizing, pulling on our bones and urging us to adventure. While he was still charmed by it, for a few months, at least, I was able to borrow my son's eyes and see the moon with a fresh vision.

As my son has grown older and has experienced the novelty of things that have become careworn to me, I have been granted this fresh vision over and over. Part of the delight of watching children mature is this rediscovery on the part of the watcher—when ordinary objects and rituals come alive for the first time for the young, they are resurrected in our own view.

This gift of sight is also part of what makes teaching so extraordinary. In my high school English class, no matter how many times I have taught a particular story or poem, the students' pleasure in the lesson helps me remember why I like the piece, why I find it valuable.

Likewise, when we discuss issues or themes, students sometimes have gifted insights or creative twists to their outlooks that are original and exciting, keeping my sojourn in the classroom from getting stale.

Some of my most creative and insightful students have been my Advanced Placement English students. Their commitment to the class begins in the spring of their junior year when I send them a copy of Homer's *Odyssey* with instructions to read it during the summer and to prepare for a test on their first day as seniors. Odysseys, with all the exploration and potential for disasters and rewards they imply, set the tone for the rest of the year as I challenge my students to think more deeply about the universal issues that emerge from our study of literature.

This year my AP students were especially playful. If they weren't always having fun, I was, and I'm convinced they have learned quite a lot since last August. Their in-class timed essays are longer and messier now because they have more to say and they try to say it better, editing themselves with numerous strikeovers and marginalia. They are more hesitant about blurting out thoughtless comments in class discussions, but they are less defensive about their positions when they do. They complain that I expect too much from them, but they brag about the workload to their peers. They call me—affectionately—Mrs. McSatan and tell me that I torment them by playing devil's advocate in every class discussion, pouncing on any stray comment that cannot be supported sufficiently, but I notice later that they watchdog their own logic better and more effectively than I can ever hope to.

These things don't happen easily or quickly. Our nine months together have been like all other gestations, incredibly painful moments followed by great joy.

My seniors graduate tomorrow. Like their peers in the rest of York County, they will walk across a stage and receive a piece of paper that symbolizes their new status as successful navigators of the land of high school. They have mastered the language, paid homage to the monuments, visited the attractions, and now are ready for new vistas. If they were lucky, they traveled with teachers who still enjoy the journey, who have the natives' affection for the familiar and the zeal to explain it to the tourists.

When my students walk across the stage tomorrow, they will also walk on out of my life. A few will send notes and drop in from time to time, and a few will return from college as fellow teachers, but most will continue their odysseys to far horizons with different companions. That's how it should be, of course, just as the moon must stop being a miracle before the two-year-old can see the rest of the sky.

Next August, I, too, will meet new companions. They will have read Homer over the summer and will bring with them a very old story, of clever Odysseus, the man who was never at a loss, and I will borrow their eyes to see him once more as a marvelous metaphor for our adventure about to begin.

THE POWER OF POETRY

April 23, 2003

APRIL IS NATIONAL POETRY MONTH. It is also the month associated with taxes and the birth of William Shakespeare, and depending on your attitude about poetry, you might think that one of those events is an apt coincidence.

In my own English classes, I rarely find any students who are neutral about poetry. They either hate it or love it, ironically for the same reasons.

"Poetry is so short and packed with meaning," both the lovers and the haters say.

Indeed. A poem is the poet's thoughts and feelings distilled into a powerful concentrate. A poem is a tightly wound spring ready to uncoil under a reader's touch.

Not just poetry in the classical or traditional sense, but all language crafted with care and passion is both an expression of the poet's ideas and a call to respond, and this is what gives it its power. Poetry lovers and poetry haters alike recognize the power of its language—some relishing it and others fearing it, but all acknowledging it.

This power is why First Lady Laura Bush canceled the Poetry and the American Voice Symposium at the White House planned for February 12. When some invited poets decided to read poetry critical of the impending war, the event was scrapped.

"It would be inappropriate to turn a literary event into a political forum," the First Lady's representative said.

American poet laureate Billy Collins told the Associated Press that "if political protest is urgent, I don't think it needs to wait for an appropriate scene and setting and should be as disruptive as it wants to be."

English poet laureate Andrew Motion said of the cancellation that "poetry ought to be part of general life rather than being ghettoized."

"Ghettoizing" war as a topic of poetry and discourse is what some critics see happening in the public schools as well. In New Mexico, two high school teachers were suspended for refusing to remove student artwork with an anti-war theme from their classrooms. Many school districts, including some local schools, have instructed their teachers not to discuss the war with students.

This tendency to ghettoize war is apparent in the protest movement, too. Some supporters of the military actions in Iraq have been vocal in their opinions that public dissent during war is inappropriate and off-limits. War protesters have been criticized, though their protests seem to have had minimal effect on the course the administration has charted in Iraq. Why then such a virulent reaction from the public?

Because the public recognizes the power of poetry and poetic language. Language is how we express our thoughts and emotions, and when a well-turned phrase expresses a thought or emotion opposed to our own, we are shaken; the less secure we are in our own beliefs, the more defensive we become.

Poetry also elicits a response from the reader. Some people advocate censorship because they recognize the power of poetry to change attitudes and behaviors. Where they err is in discounting the power of the reader to critically analyze the poetry. Instead, they are afraid that readers—or listeners—will be swayed into unthinking allegiance with the poet.

Even the most brutal regimes have recognized the power of poetry and poetic language to express and elicit responses. During the Iran-Iraq War, the Ayatollah Khomeini cautioned against unorthodox words and thoughts by warning that "the pen is mightier than the sword" in his speeches and on posters. Khomeini was so afraid of the power of language that even as Iraqi bombs were killing citizens in Tehran, the Iranian police were themselves killing others, executing dissidents whose only weapons were words.

The power of poetry and poetic language is also why would-be writers steal words. In the Italian film *Il Postino*, the barely literate postman Mario plagiarizes the poetry of Pablo Neruda to woo the beautiful niece of a local tavern owner. When Neruda confronts him about his plagiarism,

Mario says that "poetry isn't for those who write it but for those who need it." For many people like Mario, poetry belongs to the realm of the utilitarian—Hallmark cards and wedding toasts—but for others, like the tavern owner who sees her niece falling under the spell of the love poetry, "words are the worst things."

National Poetry Month is a good time to examine our beliefs about words. Are words really the worst things? Can words really "belong" to the people who say and write them, or is plagiarism pragmatism in disguise? Do people need to be protected from words? Is censorship the best way to do that? Is critical thinking the best inoculation against indoctrination? Is canceling a public forum on poetry and circumscribing what poetry is about the right way to deal with dissent? Can freedom of speech exist when people are frightened, especially when they are frightened of words and their effects?

On the other hand, April is almost over and the topic is too important for a cursory discussion. We might just have to declare a National Poetry Year.

INSPIRED DESPERATION

May 11, 2002

THOMAS EDISON was being modest when he said that "genius is one percent inspiration and 99 percent perspiration." I, however, am being truthful when I admit that the best moments in my high school English class are 99 percent perspiration and one percent desperation.

Recently one source of desperation was a migraine which left me weary and ragged after a sleepless night. At first it flickered and skittered on the edges of my consciousness, but by noon it was a child having a tantrum, demanding my full attention. When my sophomores entered the classroom, I winced as Catherine shrilly said, "Mrs. McSpadden, that story we read for homework didn't make any sense at all."

The story in question was Amy Tan's *The Rules of the Game*, a tale about a young chess prodigy who resents her mother's interference in her life. Usually I enjoy the challenge of picking up a student's verbal gauntlet and trying to make an unappreciated lesson worthwhile, but on this day the headache was taking all of my energy. Instead of launching into my typical spiel, I said, quietly so as not to hurt my own ears, "Why?"

Catherine was short and to the point.

"Because the girl's mad at her mother for being proud of her. That's dumb!"

The rest of the class had started listening to my conversation with Catherine and began to chime in.

"Yeah," April added. "The girl is really mean to her mother, and the mother didn't do anything to her."

"Yes, she did," Mary Catherine interrupted. "The mother was getting on her nerves. She acted like the girl's accomplishments were her own."

I put the safe, predictable, textbook worksheets I had planned for my class back into my desk drawer, looked at my 26 students, and asked, slowly, softly, "Is the mother in this story simply proud of her daughter, or is she living vicariously through her?" Immediately April asked what "vicariously" meant.

"Guess," I said.

They hazarded several explanations and soon puzzled it out. Then they began to debate in earnest. The class was evenly divided between those who felt the mother had every right to be proud of her daughter and those who felt the mother was using her daughter to show off to the neighbors. For almost an hour they debated passionately, pointing to specific lines and paragraphs in the story as evidence. At least twice, students suddenly saw the faults of their own logic and did loud about-faces, making us laugh. Occasionally I redirected an answer or asked another question, but mostly I sat and listened to them thinking out loud. Too soon the dismissal bell rang and the students filed out to lunch, still debating with each other.

What serendipity, I thought, to have this headache. It muzzled me and forced my students to teach the lesson.

Two days later I needed more serendipity with the same class. I was presenting Richard Wilbur's "Boy at the Window," a poem about a young boy who cries because he has left his snowman out in the storm. Ironically, the snowman is weeping too, though not for himself. The poet says in the last line of the poem that the snowman weeps because the boy is *"surrounded by such warmth, such light, such love, and so much fear."*

I was talkative, my headache long gone, but my students sat silent as stones.

"What could that line mean?" I asked, but no one spoke. I tried again.

"How could the boy live in warmth, light, love, and fear?"

Twenty-six pairs of eyes stared back. I rephrased my question four or five other ways, and each time the class was silent and wary.

And then in desperation I said, "Okay, who can tell me a story about the boy in this poem? Make up a story that explains how he can feel warmth and love and light and fear."

To my astonishment, five hands shot up immediately.

"It was a cold winter night," Jamie began, "and the little boy was sitting with his mother and father in the house beside the fireplace. Suddenly it started storming and he was really afraid."

Before I could comment, Lindsay waved her arm wildly, begging to be called on.

"See," she said, lowering her arm, "the boy took his dog to the park one day, and it was warm and light, and the boy was playing with the dog, and then the dog ran out into the road and was hit by a truck."

The class reacted in horror.

"You can't kill his dog!" Jordan admonished her, and Lindsay turned in her desk to face him.

"His dog doesn't die, but he's in the hospital, so the boy is sad now and afraid that his dog will die. But he doesn't! I wouldn't kill his dog!"

Another student told about the boy, and then another, and soon the boy at the window was transformed, Pinocchio-style, into a real boy, fleshed out by my students' stories. We eavesdropped on his family and peered through the window at the boy's life so intensely that when the bell rang, we were startled.

On the test several days later, my students wrote that the boy represents us all, with ordinary lives that are sometimes punctuated by moments of winter and desperation. Winter, they concluded, won't last forever, and desperation can lead to great empathy and insights.

And, I might add, to some pretty good English classes.

SWEETENING A SOUR SEMESTER

December 16, 2006

SOMEONE OUGHT TO WRITE a country music ballad about unrequited teaching. I'd buy it. I've just spent a semester looking encouragingly at my students' faces, hoping for some sign of joy or enthusiasm, only to be met with indifference.

Or better yet, I'd like to hear a 12-bar blues lament about the end of a semester gone sour. I'd play it on the way to work and back, seeking the kind of catharsis that only the concentrated emotions of lyrics or poetry can confer.

I became an English teacher because I love literature and composition, but I have stayed a teacher because I fell in love with teenagers. They certainly need someone to love them.

After the terrible twos, the teenage years may be the time when young humans are their least attractive. Yet watching teenagers discover their newfound brain power—the explosion in their understanding and their

229

willingness to explore the new—is thrilling. Nourishing this growth is the most important work I will ever do.

Still, this past semester I have felt like a failure more often than I have seen any success.

For example, several years ago I pulled all the dictionaries off my bookshelf and put one under each student desk, but this is the first year that my students have had to consult them constantly. Words that have baffled them? Baffle, for one. And reciprocate. Keen. Pox. Incompatible. Reveal. Typical. Significant. Casualty. Ceremonial. Snobby.

Words that should be regulars in their language toolbox are completely unknown—and consequently the thoughts those words can convey are unavailable to them. Whether I am speaking or facilitating a class discussion or directing my students' attention to the literature or returning their writing for revision, this language barrier—this vocabulary chasm—has left me a bit shaken, a bit unsteady in my confidence as a teacher. My lessons have fallen flat, my explanations have caused more confusion, and I have sat too many days in my classroom after the final bell in a self-pitying funk.

Fortunately my colleague Marian recently reminded me of a truth that all teachers need to hear from time to time, that even the small successes are worth celebrating.

Let me tell you about David and poetry.

David moved to South Carolina from Mexico several years ago and is still too shy to attempt much English. When I ask him to write and read in Spanish, he does so gladly, his deep baritone rolling across the room like a slow, silty river. When I ask him to speak in English, he goes silent.

Recently I assigned two poems for memorization to the class as preparation for the Poetry Out Loud contest in the spring. For the past two years, the National Endowment for the Arts and the Poetry Foundation have sponsored a national recitation contest for high school students. The organizers hope that the public performance of poetry will help students discover the beauty of English and the enjoyment of sharing it with an audience. This is the first year that my school has participated, and it seemed like an ideal project for public speaking students.

Like most of his peers, David rifled through the official anthologies for the shortest poems to memorize. He selected Robert Frost's "Fire and Ice" and Sara Teasdale's "Let It Be Forgotten" and began to work on them with the district ESOL teacher once a week. On the day of the recitation, David spoke softly and shyly, giving Robert Frost's careworn poem about the different ways that relationships can end—in icy indifference or fiery anger—a sadness that made the class of wriggly sophomores unusually quiet, as if they were holding their breath.

When he finished, David glanced at me and then began reciting his second poem.

> Let it be forgotten, as a flower is forgotten,
> Forgotten as a fire that once was singing gold.
> Let it be forgotten forever and ever,
> Time is a kind friend, he will make us old.

If anyone asks, say it was forgotten
Long and long ago,
As a flower, as a fire, as a hushed footfall
In a long-forgotten snow.

The gentleness in David's voice made Sara Teasdale's poem unbearably wistful. As the last word died away, the class clapped and whistled, and Robert, who had mangled the same two poems earlier, yelled out enthusiastically, "You are bilingual, man! You make me look BAD!"

The whole thing took two minutes, three, perhaps, moments when I felt the class and I were floating and buoyant at last, moments I almost forgot in the overwhelming tide of the semester.

LESSONS

October 7, 2006

EACH YEAR when I finally stop grieving for summer and my students settle into a routine, I take a deep breath and look at my state of the union. Next week marks the end of the first grading period, and I am only now taking time to sort through the successes and the failures, the lessons learned and the lessons lost so far. As usual I realize that my students are teaching me more than I am teaching them—a timeworn adage, to be sure—but this year I have the disturbing sense that I am a slow learner, that the lessons they are teaching me are the same ones that I have to relearn year after year.

My seniors are teaching me that every student deserves to be seen as an individual. The two sets of identical twins in my Advanced Placement English class are seeing to that. For the first month of school I spent an incredible amount of energy observing the twins and looking for ways to tell them apart. At least Katherine and Elizabeth Podmore are mirror twins—Elizabeth is left-handed and Katherine is right-handed—but that isn't helpful unless I see them pick up a pen. Aerin and Aubrey Phillips are both right-handed, so I have to look for differences in the parts in their hair (Aubrey's is straighter than Aerin's) or in the way they hold their pencils (Aerin loops her thumb over her forefinger).

Finally after two months I am starting to see more subtle distinctions in the way they stride forward or hold back, their deference to one twin to speak first, the differences in the level of anxiety in their glance. But I am not naturally observant and my poor brain is often befuddled when I hand back papers or see the girls separately in the hall.

"Don't worry," Katherine—or maybe Elizabeth—reassures me often. "You are doing better than most of our teachers."

My other class of seniors, a group of at-risk students with various learning disabilities, are not only reteaching me the importance of seeing students as individuals, but they are challenging me to see beyond their limitations. Though none of them are fluent readers, all of them are tackling the daunting British literature textbook with reasonable grace and good humor.

Their difficulty interpreting written text can make them appear dull and lazy, but in fact each one—even the most handicapped—is a capable thinker. On a recent essay test about Shakespeare's *Much Ado About Nothing*, for example, I asked them to speculate about why one of the main characters, Beatrice, turns down the prince's proposal of marriage. Some echoed what Beatrice herself implies, that she is not in the same class as the prince, but many also included their opinion that, contrary to what Beatrice says, she is still in love with another man, something we had not discussed as a class but which Beatrice's later actions confirm.

Most poignant of all was one girl's response. During the test she raised her hand and called me over to take issue with the question. She was hunched over in her desk, sniffling with one of her frequent colds, bundled in the same torn clothes she wears every other day.

"This part of the play isn't realistic," she said, and when I asked her what she meant, she went on. "No poor person like Beatrice is going to turn down marriage to a rich person like a prince."

My last class each day is a group of sophomores taking creative writing. Like most sophomores, they are, indeed, "wise fools." On good days they teach me patience. On bad days they simply tax it. They are noisy and silly and at times thoughtlessly cruel to each other.

Yet when we started our unit on poetry I sensed the beginnings of empathy. More than any other genre, poetry is where my students reveal their heartaches. They can be flippant in their short stories or hide behind their characters when they write their plays, but modern poetry demands an honesty that even a 15-year-old respects.

In their poems they tell of the hurt of divorce and death. They write about moving far from home and losing their sense of belonging. They tell about injustices they have committed and their wonder that they have been for-given or their grief that they haven't been.

When they read their poems to the class, I learn again that I love teaching.

It can be a hard lesson to hold on to some days.

But it is the lesson that keeps me steady, that sends me back into the classroom every year.

BANNED BOOKS

August 24, 2001

TWO YEARS AGO both of my sons, then aged thirteen and eleven, managed to get copies of two banned books and read them. I know, because the books were gifts from me.

I gave my younger son, a somewhat reluctant reader, *Harry Potter and the Sorcerer's Stone*, hoping that the fantasy world would intrigue him enough to get him to read more. Not only did he quickly read the rest of the series, but the books were a welcome respite from his own middle school struggles with schoolyard bullies, and he found great comfort in Harry's ability to persevere against evil.

I gave my older son, a serious child who thinks deeply about history and social issues, Harper Lee's *To Kill a Mockingbird*. Although the book is a mature, tragic examination of the consequences of racism, I hoped that, despite his youth, he would be able to broaden his understanding of the tensions of race and culture that he has unwittingly

237

inherited as a Southern white boy. Fortunately, that year his English class read the book together and spent many hours in discussions and seminars fueled by his gifted and enthusiastic teacher, a black woman who treasured the novel as an indictment against prejudice and as a celebration of bravery and compassion.

Both novels, banned in certain school districts throughout the country, have served my sons well, doing what good literature does—connecting us through words to the rest of humanity. No matter what our own peculiar situations, great books unite us as members of a larger tribe, resonating with the universal experiences that we all share—experiences of joy and sorrow, love and hate, good and evil.

Not everyone agrees that literature either can or should do this—particularly literature which, like the Harry Potter books or Lee's *To Kill a Mockingbird*, has some challenged content or language.

Most censors are probably motivated from a genuine worry about exposing readers—particularly young ones— to what they themselves find immoral or disturbing, but others, especially elected officials, have been more self-serving by calling for the removal of controversial books from libraries and schools, hoping to quiet any complaints among their constituents.

Especially troubling is the recent situation in Muskogee, Oklahoma, where the school board voted to remove *To Kill a Mockingbird* from the required reading list for freshmen after several students and their parents complained about the novel's use of the word "nigger." In explaining the removal, board member Muriel Saunders told reporters that "unless someone's walked in our shoes, they can't really understand what things mean to us."

She's right, of course, that being black in America is different from being white, but she's wrong to suggest that silence is a better solution than dialogue.

Early in the novel, the main character, lawyer Atticus Finch, shares Muriel Saunders' concerns when he tells his six-year-old daughter, "If you learn a single trick, Scout, you'll get along a lot better with all kinds of folks. You never really understand a person until you consider things from his point of view—until you climb into his skin and walk around in it."

When National Public Radio's Melissa Block asked Muriel Saunders in an interview if she realized that she was echoing Atticus' advice to Scout, Saunders bristled that she was speaking from unhappy personal experiences with Jim Crow laws and discrimination, "not from something I read."

If she had read the novel and had let it speak to her, she could have, in those darker moments of despair, felt a little less lonely.

The students at Muskogee High can still choose to read *To Kill a Mockingbird*—it hasn't been banned, only removed from the required reading list—but if they are like the teenagers I know, "optional book" means no book at all, and Harper Lee's heartbreaking tale of justice denied and lessons painfully gathered will go unread, untaught, unlearned.

All censors recognize the power of language to hurt—indeed, we all act as though the pen really is mightier than the sword when we argue for or against particular books in the canon—but sometimes hurtful words or provocative topics help us see our way clear to a helpful or healing perspective. *To Kill a Mockingbird* is a book that can do just that—but only if it is read.

That's why the Chicago Public Library has recently added it to its "One Book, One Chicago" citywide reading program. Commissioner Mary Dempsey said that she hopes the novel will "stimulate discussions across cultural, class, and racial lines."

The school board members in Muskogee were unimpressed.

"You can't compare Muskogee with Chicago," Muriel Saunders said. People in Muskogee, she went on to say, are slow to change.

My own sons have been quick to change before my eyes from small children who benefited from my censoring their TV, movies, and toys, to curious teenagers ready to read the banned books I handed them.

We are fooling ourselves if we think we can protect children forever from the ugliness of the world. What we can do is give them some guidance as they discover it, helping them grow into adults willing to work together to understand each other, willing to walk around inside each other's skins.

BLOCKBUSTERS

July 16, 2005

THIRTY YEARS AGO THIS SUMMER, movie audiences hunkered down in their theater seats and shivered with delicious fright. *Jaws*, Steven Spielberg's masterful retelling of *Moby Dick*, cast a great white shark instead of a great white whale as the threatening sea creature, but the other major characters were the same—the crazy captain, the level-headed first mate, the naive landlubber—and the danger was just as thrilling. The movie soon broke box office attendance records.

It also quickly broke financial records. Made for $12 million, *Jaws* went on to gross over $250 million, a profit margin that at first seemed unbelievable. That unbelievable profit soon became not only believable but also required as Hollywood studio executives searched for the next big hit—and the blockbuster mentality was born. Independent filmmakers who struggled to get their modest projects funded after the summer of 1975 may have felt that the great white shark had attacked them personally.

As much as I admire Steven Spielberg and enjoy *Jaws*, I can't help but feel that as moviegoers we have been impoverished by their success. You can't blame investors for wanting the largest return on their money, nor can you blame audiences for enjoying the large, noisy canvases of popular genre films. Yet moviegoers who prefer a bit of art instead of mere entertainment with their popcorn have found the pickings slim in the multiplexes.

Nor is film the only literary medium to succumb to money fever. The book publishing industry is also on a constant search for the next blockbuster novel—or better yet, the next blockbuster writer, someone who has his pulse on the mass market and can appeal to the most readers. Barnes and Noble even has a spot on its website where readers can ask to be notified when their favorite author has a new book pending.

As much as I admire many authors and enjoy reading, I can't help but feel that as book lovers we are impoverished by this cult of celebrity. Especially troubling is the newest practice of pre-selling books by particular authors—asking readers to buy books sight unseen regardless of their merits.

Yet earlier this week I finally gave in and plunked down my money, and today I will stand in line with many, many other people to pick up my copy of *Harry Potter and the Half-Blood Prince*. J. K. Rowling's track record with the other five Harry Potter novels is comforting—I loved them all and will undoubtedly love this one—but I also know that what *Jaws* did for filmmaking, Harry Potter has helped do for publishing. In 1997 Rowling struggled to find a publisher for her first edition of *Harry Potter and the Philosopher's Stone*, and only 500 copies were printed. By contrast, over ten million copies of her newest novel have already been printed, with many more millions anticipated—a summer blockbuster indeed.

My ambivalence about Steven Spielberg and J. K. Rowling is not a reflection of their work. They enrich our culture in a positive way, and they have afforded many people, including me, much pleasure and education into the human condition. However, I worry that the quieter diverse voices—the quirky, funky, offbeat movies and books that might appeal to smaller audiences—are being silenced, and all of us are poorer for their loss.

Still, I'm hopeful. On a recent trip to Blockbuster Video, I was shocked by the number of foreign language and niche-market films displayed on the new arrival shelf. A decade ago a salesclerk had warned as I was renting *My Dinner With André*, a movie about two New Yorkers discussing the theater, "Don't take this one. We're getting rid of it because everyone complains about it when they bring it back."

"It's okay," I assured him. "I've seen it before."

The clerk raised an incredulous eyebrow.

"And you liked it? Go figure."

That same Blockbuster today stocks *The Five Obstructions*, a movie I bought two months ago from Amazon because I was certain it would never turn up for rental.

Featuring two Danish filmmakers discussing their art, the movie is charming and fascinating and intensely cerebral, the kind of anti-blockbuster that deserves its small but appreciative audience.

The growing popularity of the Sundance Film Festival—started three years after the summer of *Jaws*—or the more aggressive distribution and marketing of foreign films—or perhaps a jaded audience looking for something different may be behind Blockbuster's decision to devote precious space to unusual films such as *The Five Obstructions*. I'm hoping that similar forces will come to bear on the book publishers soon. As much as I love my blockbuster novels—and I will probably do little else this week except immerse myself in Hogwarts with Harry Potter—I like hearing from other authors, too, whose point of view might be startling or challenging, whose words require me to stretch my understanding of the world and my place in it.

THE HERO'S JOURNEY

May 19, 1999

THE WAITING ROOM WAS SMALL and the woman was loud, but I didn't start eavesdropping in earnest until she mentioned *Star Wars*.

"*Star Wars* was so popular when it came out because all the other movies were sleazy and violent," the mother asserted.

Her teenaged son, hunched over miserably with a streaming cold, replied, "Luke Skywalker killed about a million people when he blew up the Death Star. That's pretty violent."

Before his mother could comment, he went on. "I thought *Star Wars* was so popular because it showed a traditional hero—you know, good versus evil and all that jazz."

I mentally high-fived the teenager and thought about my own English students.

For the past few years my senior Advanced Placement English students and I have begun our study of world literature with a discussion about *Star Wars* and whether it qualifies as mythology. By his own account, George Lucas was influenced by scholar Joseph Campbell's 1973 publication of *The Hero With A Thousand Faces*, an elegant argument for the universality of heroes and the hero cycle in mythology, folklore, and religion.

By examining hero stories from multiple times and cultures, Campbell concluded that our common human experiences have given rise to similar legends everywhere. Ultimately, Campbell said, the hero's journey echoes our own journey through life.

After we discuss *Star Wars* and mythology, my seniors and I spend the rest of the year considering how literature in general—the accounts of the hero's journey—is relevant to our own lives. Those stories which are most meaningful are the ones in which the hero's struggles are our struggles: developing a unique identity, exploring relationships with other people, finding a sense of purpose and fulfillment.

Literature which does not resonate with these universal concerns of truth and appearance, justice and mercy, love and hate, good and evil will be read once and forgotten, irrelevant amusements which teach us little about ourselves. Novels and films which center around a current gimmick, no matter how clever, will not speak to the next generation once the gimmick is gone.

On the other hand, literature which teaches and delights will be translated across cultures and through time.

Witness the current hot author in Hollywood—William Shakespeare—a man dead for almost 400 years whose strength was not in creating magnificent stories from nothing but who borrowed liberally from myths and legends popular in his day. Those myths and legends were relevant then and are relevant now because they are about us.

Some critics have objected to calling *Star Wars* a modern myth, words freighted with religious overtones. Indeed, devoted fans and ardent critics often sound like threatened zealots—read the back-and-forth defenses and assaults on the newest *Star Wars* movie, *The Phantom Menace.* Cartoons depict costumed moviegoers being jeered at by ordinary suburbanites who tell them to "get a life." *Star Wars* enthusiasts bicker with sports fans about whose entertainment is more meaningful.

But people have always searched for meaning in many places. In preliterate days they went to shamans or medicine men to interpret the confusing world around them. Myths and legends arose to pass these explanations on and were formalized into religious practices.

In those early myths, heroes such as Beowulf were physically strong and able to slay monsters because the myth makers themselves led difficult lives shortened by animal predators and devastating illnesses. In more civilized parts of the world, heroes were intelligent people who could outwit villains when they couldn't outfight them—heroes such as the Greek Odysseus.

Yet, Odysseus is more like Beowulf than he is different. They each wrestle with the forces of evil, are self-sacrificing, and despite their determination to succeed, sometimes fail. In other words, they live on a grand scale the ordinary experiences we all face.

Modern heroes have evolved, also, and like the myths before them, they are both universal and particular. The current debate about whether popular culture is a cause of society's values or a reflection of them is a misdirected one; our myths and our values are an interlocking spiral. People today do as people always have done—create myths and literature as an expression of who we are. In turn, we emulate those heroes and pattern our journeys after theirs.

In this century recognizable heroes often have been hard to find, either in real life or in our literature. Instead, modern novels and films offer us ambiguous heroes, none so sympathetic that we mourn their suffering, none so unsympathetic that we hope for their demise. Against this jaded and somewhat cynical backdrop, George Lucas has offered viewers an unabashedly symbolic and mythic story. Critics may dismiss it as derivative or bemoan the marketing hype, missing the reason for its mysterious pull and sense of collective sacrament.

The teenager in the doctor's office got it right. The story works because it is about heroes and good and evil and all that jazz.

TALES

January 27, 2001

PETER O'TOOLE is having a tantrum, acting circles around Richard Burton who stares stony-faced into the distance. They are Henry II and Thomas Becket, friends turned enemies in the year 1170, and despite the glare from the overhead fluorescent lights, my students and I can see them heading to the inevitable murder in Canterbury Cathedral.

Or, at least most of my students can. When I stop the film every few minutes to ask questions—"Why did Becket do that?" or "What do you think will happen now?"—I see that one, then two, and then three students have put their heads down.

"I just can't watch old movies like this," Erin says when I poke her awake, and I know what she means. At 151 minutes, *Becket* is an hour longer than the movies these teenagers pay $6 to see every weekend, and their attention spans poop out long before the story reaches the climax.

Worse, I am showing it on a TV set, technology so ordinary and ignorable after thousands of hours of slack-jawed watching that it has become just another buzz in the background electric chorus of air conditioners, dishwashers, hair dryers. At home my students use TV to lull them to sleep at night; at school they struggle to stay awake whenever I turn one on.

Some of my students come to the movie's defense, but they are the exceptions. I go home that day feeling like the worst teacher in the world.

I had chosen to show *Becket* as an introduction to *The Canterbury Tales*, Chaucer's medieval masterpiece that reads like a cross between a tabloid gossip magazine and a serious social commentary. The bulk of the book is a series of short stories supposedly told by a group of religious pilgrims as they travel to the shrine of the murdered Thomas Becket at Canterbury Cathedral, but the introductory Prologue which paints delightfully irreverent pictures of the pilgrims themselves is what my students will study. Now, after the movie fiasco, I am leery about leaping into a poem 1000 lines long.

So I hesitate.

Instead, I tell my students to close their books and listen.

"Once upon a time," I begin, and as I look at the faces of this class of seniors, many who have failed English in the past, many who work long hours after school, I realize that for the first time since I met them at the beginning of the new semester, I have everyone's attention.

I tell them Chaucer's "The Wife of Bath's Tale," the

story of a Crusader whose sentence of death for raping a virgin is commuted upon the condition that he finds out within one year the answer to this question: What do women want most? The students who slept through the bloody screen stabbing of Thomas Becket are wide-awake.

The knight, I tell my students, can't believe what an easy sentence he has been given—until he begins asking women for the answer. One woman says that money is what women really want; another says children; still another assures the knight that women want fun in bed. My students are laughing wildly, but they quiet down when I describe the knight's distress as he heads back to court a year later and not a day smarter.

Then I step into the story and become the ugly hag the knight meets in the forest, the one who exchanges the correct answer for a promise of a favor.

"I'll bet she makes him marry her!" Erin says.

Of course her prediction is right, and the students squeal when I tell how the knight was forced to marry the old hag after he revealed the correct answer: What women want most is to be the boss, to have their way, to make the decisions.

I sit back on my desk that has become the honeymoon bed and tell the knight that I am not really an ugly hag but a bewitched princess. I can be beautiful again, but then I will be unfaithful and make the knight miserable with jealousy. Or I can remain as I am, wrinkled, smelly, drooling, and I will keep a clean home and cook good food and offer intelligent conversation.

"Which do you prefer?" I ask, and the class and I savor the dilemma.

"Now," I say, "this knight had learned his lesson at last, so he turned to his ugly hag of a wife and told her to choose which way she would be, either beautiful and faithless or ugly and faithful. After all, she was the boss."

The class applauds when the hag rewards the knight for her freedom by choosing to be beautiful and faithful, and I go home feeling like the best teacher in the world.

That night one of my students shares "The Wife of Bath's Tale" with his father who never finished high school.

Later, when he tells me about it, I can picture this student, who told me the first day of school that he has always hated English, bringing Chaucer alive as a gift for his dad, a gift offered out of genuine love and not out of the smugness of a performance well appreciated, and I know that I am looking at the real best teacher in the world.

CHOICES

May 25, 2000

MY STUDENTS are annoyed with the butler.

He is the quintessential English butler who tempers his impulses and hides his feelings.

They are typical American teenagers who can't imagine doing either.

For them, honest, loud, immediate self-expression is a virtue. They choose to express their annoyance with me, also, loudly and immediately, for making them read Kazuo Ishiguro's *The Remains of the Day*, a Booker Prize novel about Stevens, an aging butler who realizes too late that his life has been wasted through foolish choices.

My students aren't annoyed with Stevens for making foolish choices. They confess, with almost gleeful honesty, to their own stupid gaffes and goofy decisions. What annoys them about the butler, and what baffles, them, too, is that his foolish choices have permanent consequences, that despite his best efforts and strongest wishes, Stevens must learn to live with the unhappy results of what he has done.

Their irritation with him is a testament to their belief in the power of free will. They are adamant that, unlike Stevens, they would never work for an unworthy employer or hesitate to voice their opinions. Why, they want to know, doesn't he just act on his feelings instead of thinking so much? Why, for instance, doesn't he just tell the housekeeper that he loves her?

"She's married to someone else now and has a daughter," I remind them. "He can't ask her to leave her family."

"But they love each other," they protest, and to that, all I can say is, "It's too late."

"Too late" is a term that mystifies them. As teenagers, they have made few decisions that they can't easily unmake, and their optimism about the future is one of their great charms and their greatest vulnerability.

At some level they seem to know this—as graduation looms in the next few days, the choices they have made about working hard or slacking off in high school have caught up with them as scholarship offers and college acceptances appear in the mail—or don't. For the first time in their lives they have a real say in where they will live and what they will be doing after graduation. My seniors have started to realize that their decisions about work and school and relationships will shape what happens tomorrow, and they ask, "What if I pick the wrong thing?"

What, indeed?

As we continue to discuss the novel, a few of my students comment that some of their peers have already made decisions that can't be reversed. Several of their friends have babies. One is married. Many are working in after-school jobs that will become their lifetime careers. Others haven't passed the courses necessary to graduate and may never get meaningful work. All of them know students who have died because someone chose to drink and drive.

When they talk about the adults in their lives, they recognize that many are still reeling from long-ago decisions that have led to drug addiction and disease, soured marriages and divorces, disappointing careers and difficult offspring.

Yet even as they strain to peer into their futures, my seniors keep hoping that somehow they will be exempt from any truly nasty mistakes, that disaster will spare them, that they will not come to the end of their lives and say, as Stevens must say, "If only I had done things differently."

I don't want to squash my students' idealism or make them feel defeated, but I do want them to sympathize with the people they will meet whose response to tragedy is to endure rather than to rage. I want them to understand that sometimes people shrive themselves for their own missteps by staying the course instead of fleeing the scene. I want them to hold on to their hope while learning to be more cautious, more aware of the forever aspect of what they decide today.

On the final test for *The Remains of the Day*, I include a playful question that is designed to measure this broader perspective. I ask my students to prove that this novel about an old English butler has something to teach American teenagers.

They do so handily. Although they were annoyed with the butler before, now they can imagine their own upcoming decisions going awry; if they were inclined to be judgmental in the past, their identification with Stevens, however fleeting, has encouraged them to be kinder to those in need of forgiveness.

"This book is about a man whose heart is at war with his head," one insightful student writes, and if there is a better way to express the source of so much human misery, I don't know what it is.

It also expresses the angst of teenagers whose grand task is learning to balance the impulses of the heart with the dreams of the mind, using them as twin compasses to chart their journeys, arriving at the remains of their days glad for the destinations they have chosen.

A LOVE SONNET

February 14, 2001

IT'S FEBRUARY, so we are studying Shakespeare—the romantic comedies *Much Ado About Nothing* and *Twelfth Night* and the darkly tragic *Macbeth*—and as we approach Valentine's Day, we read the love sonnets.

A month into the new semester and my English IV seniors and I have left behind the Anglo-Saxons and the Dark Ages of Britain, plowing ahead through the Renaissance. My students have been politely bored with the poetry of Sidney, relieved by the simple vocabulary of Spenser, mildly amused by the cavorting nymphs and shepherds of Marlowe and Raleigh, but not until we read Shakespeare's sonnets does anyone get mad.

"What do you think about this?" I ask, and I read from Sonnet 116, *Love is not love which alters when it alteration finds.*

No one says a word.

"What's Shakespeare talking about?" I prod. Still no one speaks. The class and I play a game of chicken to see who will break down and give an answer first. We lock stares and wait.

Finally someone asks, "What does alteration mean," and I tell them to read the line again using the word "change" for "alter" and "alteration."

"That doesn't make any sense," Aleigha pronounces. "Love is not love which changes when it change finds."

But several students suddenly do understand the line. They all start to speak at once, Luke talking loudest of all.

"I know, I know, I know!" he says. "True love doesn't stop just because someone changes."

"So," I say, going back to my original question, "what do you think about this?"

"Shakespeare's right," Luke says. "If you really love someone, you never stop loving them."

But he is shouted down.

"That's crazy," Rachael tells him. "I used to really really really love my boyfriend, but I don't like him even one little bit now."

The class erupts with personal sagas of faithless ex-boyfriends and ex-girlfriends. If only Shakespeare had known the people they know, they assure me, he wouldn't have written such a nutty sonnet.

"But can't you continue to love people even when they let you down, when they hurt you?" I ask, and the class quiets down. They have been hurt often and sometimes brutally by the people they love. More than one student has spoken and written about physical and emotional abuse that has destroyed their families. Some have seen violence that has led to the death of relatives and friends. Some live such chaotic days that they are never quite certain where they will spend their nights. My question is not an abstraction to them.

"Well," Cassie says slowly, clearly thinking aloud, "if you've been married to someone for a long time, if you really know them, then you can keep loving them."

I tell them that Shakespeare had that exact experience, that after living apart from his family most of his adult life, he retired from London to Stratford, presumably living again with his wife.

"You mean she just took him back?" Aleigha asks incredulously. "Didn't you say these sonnets were written for his girlfriend? Do we have any sonnets he wrote to his wife?"

I tell them I don't know. The class grumbles. A few students say, "I wouldn't take him back" and "I couldn't love anyone like that."

Then, in one of those odd moments that sometimes happens when people in a crowd stop talking at exactly the same awkward moment, the room becomes still and silent, silent enough for a young mother's soft voice to be heard.

"Parents love their children like that," she says.

No one was happy when she revealed her unplanned pregnancy last year—not her parents, not her boyfriend, not her teachers, and least of all herself. She was bewildered and perilously close to dropping out of school, tripped up by the stumbling block she had placed in her own path.

As she listens to Shakespeare's valentine of unconditional love, she may be thinking about how her own parents set aside their disappointment and helped her stay in school instead of letting her compound one mistake with another. She may be thinking of her own young son and the sacrifice she makes for him daily by leaving him and coming to school, learning English and history and math, but really learning the powerful art of self-reflection. Perhaps she is thinking of both, the past and the future, and realizing that at the too-young age of 17 years old she has discovered a great human secret, that the passion and lust and desperate romantic appetite of lovers seems shallow compared to the all-consuming selfless devotion of parents.

Now she sits in my English IV class, a senior about to graduate in a few months, a mother with a year-old son and a teenaged husband, and she says, softly, "Parents love their children like that."

And everyone, even the most cynical and skeptical among us, silently says, "Amen."

THE
EXAMINED
LIFE

A BOOMER LOOKS BACK

December 17, 2005

I DIDN'T LEARN everything I needed to know in kindergarten. I even learned some things I wish I didn't know, such as how to be frightened on stage.

That comes as a surprise to people who know me. I'm an extrovert, a yakker at the faculty lunch table, an eager smart aleck when the occasion calls for it—and even when it doesn't—someone whose report cards were always marked "talks too much." I stand up in front of a classroom of teenagers every day and feel no fear. But put me on a stage and I stutter and stumble and struggle to keep from getting sick.

I learned to be afraid on May 31, 1962, the day I graduated from kindergarten.

The story really starts the day before, when my teacher sat my classmates and me in a semicircle of diminutive chairs on the stage.

"Tomorrow," Mrs. Tribble said, "you will get your diplomas, and I want to warn you about something. Many of you will be getting new shoes, and those new shoes are going to be slick on the bottom. I want you to go home today and tell your mothers to put masking tape on the bottoms of your shoes so you won't slip on this waxed floor. Don't forget!"

That's the most ridiculous thing I've ever heard, I remember thinking.

"Hubris," I tell my students, "is pride so smug that it invites a downfall."

Then I describe my five year-old self, arms akimbo, convinced that her teacher is a barking lunatic, confident in her ability to pilot her way across a newly-waxed stage while wearing slick-bottomed patent leather Mary Janes.

You can see where this is going.

When I was called to receive my diploma, I hopped up so fast, fell so swiftly, and cried so loudly that Mrs. Tribble grabbed me by the wrist and force marched me off the stage.

I laugh when I tell this story now, but even so I feel sorry for that prideful little girl. Go back, I want to say to her. This time listen to your teacher.

But neither humility nor foresight were in the curriculum of my kindergarten. I know, because just the other day I came across the typed program my mother had saved from graduation and it listed the seven virtues the school wanted to instill in its pupils: reverence, true patriotism, courtesy, appreciation, responsibility, learning, and sharing.

The Asbury Memorial Methodist Church Kindergarten in Charleston, SC, was established in 1951 because the first wave of Baby Boomers were turning five that year. Those children were taught the same seven virtues that were the emphasis when my class graduated a decade later. To me they seem odd choices—valuable behaviors to cultivate when your world is threatened by the Cold War, perhaps, but not as profound or important to the human heart as honesty and personal integrity, courage and perseverance, empathy and compassion, humility and kindness.

"We shall watch the progress of these little friends with continued interest and affection," the kindergarten program goes on to say, and I have the same feeling reading it that I have when I tell my story about graduation. Turn back, I want to tell those children, still innocent. Go back, I want to tell the first graduates of Asbury Methodist, those first Baby Boomers, the ones who turn 60 years old this coming year, the ones who were sophomores in high school in 1962.

A Soviet spy would be released that year in exchange for U-2 pilot Gary Powers, and James Bond would continue to be a hero in books and on the screen. Thousands would protest when James Meredith integrated Old Miss, but the movie *To Kill a Mockingbird* would win rave reviews. Forty-six soldiers would be dead by the end of the year in the growing quagmire of Vietnam, yet the government would insist we were there only as advisors.

"We shall watch the progress of these little friends," the program says, and I know what those teachers and parents cannot know. I know what is ahead of those first Baby Boomers and the others my age—hard choices about war and race, about women and work, about traditional values and the counter culture. Be careful, I want to tell them.

I want to warn them about the coming turbulence, about the Cuban missile crisis and the Tet offensive and Kent State and the assassinations of the 1960s. I ache knowing that their peaceful protests will turn violent, that political scandals will forever shake their trust in authority. I want to whisper encouragement as they register voters, volunteer for the Peace Corps, return home from the war.

I want to go back to May 1962 and walk nimbly across the stage. I want to seek out the gaze of the Baby Boomers sitting in the audience. Close your eyes, I want to shout to them. This will hurt, I want to tell them. It will be over before you know it, I want to say.

TRANSFORMATIONS

December 21, 2000

I CALL IT the Christmas tree syndrome, the way that all Christmas trees on all Christmas tree lots are beautiful and perfect from the road, sturdy sentinels that as soon as I park my car and walk among them wither into fatigued veterans with gnarled branches like arthritic fingers and twisted spines which guarantee a difficult perch for the star. Trees still baled in nets are even more alluring, yet every year I am discouraged when patient tree salesmen humor me by unveiling them and twirling them slowly for my inspection, as if I were some connoisseur of evergreens.

Not just Christmas trees, but so much in life suffers from careful examination. People, places, and objects we desire are often easy to admire from afar and difficult to appreciate up close, their faults and warps and quirks exposed under our critical inspection.

I've been thinking about the Christmas tree syndrome

quite a bit lately, and not just because it is December. This year, for the first time since my high school adopted block scheduling, the fall semester ends when the students leave for the holidays. In the past, the semester ended in mid-January and the students changed to four new classes with four new teachers. By then Christmas was a fading memory, and the chilly, dreary days of January were appropriate, somehow, for goodbyes. But not this year. This year when we head off to our separate celebrations, I will know that I may not see many of my students again, and that has made me think about the time I first met them way back in August.

In many ways, meeting my students reminds me of picking out a Christmas tree and the disillusionment that comes with a final selection. When I do decide on a Christmas tree, I always feel that I am making a compromise, and as I drive home with my tree tied firmly to the top of my van, my sense of dissatisfaction grows as I notice how symmetrical, how flush and green the trees are in every lot I pass.

Likewise, on the first day of school, each new class is like a tree lot framed through the windshield—distant, quiet, seemingly ideal. During the rest of that first week, my students and I begin to see each other more clearly, our spindly deformities and prickly places apparent as we get to know each other. Establishing the class rules and struggling with discipline are always as tough as wrestling an oversized fir into a tree stand and hoping, hoping, that it doesn't come toppling over.

But the Christmas tree syndrome means a transformation, too. Each tree that I call my own begins as an unrealistic vision, becomes disappointingly real, and then changes once again into a symbol of the season, joyous and genuine. As soon as the aroma of the sap rejuvenates the stale air of the house, I stop fretting over the odd spaces between the crooked branches and see them as challenges instead. The lights and ornaments and tinsel turn every year's tree into the most beautiful tree in the world, and finally my appreciation becomes authentic—love with open eyes.

Every new class of students undergoes this transformation as well, becoming special and treasured, no matter how rascally or lazy or silly they can be at times.

So this Christmas I am sad they are leaving, after all the effort to see them as they are and to love them anyway. December is over too soon, the Christmas tree is sent off to become pulp, and my students that I have decked with term papers and class discussions and heated debates and poetry and essays and short stories leave for other classes and other teachers.

On the first day back after Christmas, many will pop their heads into my doorway between classes to say hello or to show me something they have written or simply to wave and grin, but they will no longer by my students, my class, and their absence will be palpable for awhile, the way the corner of my room at home will look oddly dark without twinkling lights and plastic icicles, the echo of the tree still there, with piles of wrapped gifts still unopened, promising treasures inside.

RESOLUTIONS

January 13, 2007

Two days before Christmas the side of my parked car was crumpled in a hit and run accident. I've tried to mitigate my anger, as people do, with the mantra that "it could have been worse." The car could have been totaled, I could have been driving it, someone could have been hurt. I've tried to be grateful that it happened when my sons were home from college and could ferry me back and forth to the body shop. I've tried to be glad that the rental company assigned me a loaner car nicer than the one that was hit.

But I'm not.

Or at least, not very.

Even when life is going smoothly I'm not very good with gratitude. Gratitude implies a lack of self-sufficiency, a vulnerability, that makes me uncomfortable. It forces me to step outside of myself long enough to notice and then acknowledge other people. Being thoughtless and oblivious is far easier.

That's why my New Year's resolution is to offer more gratitude to the people in my life who often go overlooked. Here are my first ten thank you's of 2007.

Thank you to the insurance adjusters for shrinking a major problem into a minor annoyance, for answering my calls promptly, for lowering my deductible.

Another major problem turned into a minor annoyance recently when Danny, my plumber, called me at work when he unboxed my new dishwasher and realized the supply store had delivered the wrong one. He took the wrong one back to the store and then drove twenty miles to another town to a store that had the right model without charging me anything to do it. He should get at least a thanks.

Thank you to my pharmacist, Michelle, who with utter grace telephoned the pharmacy in Georgia where my son goes to college to transfer his prescriptions to South Carolina knowing she would have to transfer them back at the end of the monthlong holiday break.

I want to extend my deepest gratitude to all the drivers in Charlotte and the surrounding areas who let me merge into crowded lanes, who stop so I can turn left in front of them, who don't honk or yell or gesture when they are tempted. To the driver of the white truck in my blind spot that I almost hit on I-77 South at rush hour, I owe you an apology as well as a thank you. Your good-natured shrug when I righted my car out of your way has made me a more careful driver.

Kudos to my mail deliverer whose route is so long that she has to drive it in the dark.

Gracias to my friend Burwell in Richmond who changed the heading on his photo Christmas card to read Happy New Year and which my mail deliverer put in my box late on January 6, inspiring me to recast my own unsent Christmas cards as Valentines.

I am thankful for the countless people in the service industry—the waiters and sales clerks and bank tellers and office receptionists—who smile even when they are weary.

My warmest appreciation for every single person waiting in the massive security line at Newark Airport on January 1 when my son Jamie was dashing from Terminal C to Terminal A to catch a flight to Berlin after his plane from Charlotte was delayed two hours. You saw and heard a frantic young man beg to jump the line and each and every one of you let him. After all that—after the delay and the lines and the mad dash to the gate—my son arrived after his plane had been sealed and the ramp was pulled away. Still, you might like to know that your sacrifice wasn't in vain. Moved, perhaps, by that same look of horror and despair on my son's face that I remember from his childhood when his knob of ice cream tumbled out of its cone onto the sidewalk, the attendant at the gate redeployed the ramp and let my son embark.

To Kat, who vacuums my classroom every day and never complains about the snow of notebook paper holes or the wadded up Kleenexes shoved under the desks, thank you, thank you, thank you.

And to Suzanne, one of my seniors, who greeted me the first day back from the holiday with a mournful, "I only get to have you four more months! That's the worst part of this semester!"—I hope I can learn what you have already mastered, how to imbue my gratitude with such kindness that it lifts someone into the air.

EPIPHANIES

January 6, 2000

WHEN MY YOUNGEST SON was assigned the role of shepherd in the annual Christmas pageant for the fourth year in a row, he mutinied. Shepherds, he explained to the director, are lowest in the pageant hierarchy. They wear bathrobes, carry sticks, and retire early to a corner of the stage with their cardboard sheep. The role he was lobbying for was one of the Magi—one of the wise men mentioned in the New Testament book of Matthew—who wears a red and purple embroidered cape, carries a gold spray-painted box and several ornate bottles, and processes down the center aisle of the church spotlighted by the star of Bethlehem at the climax of the play.

In the real world the story of the three wise men is a much quieter, even unremarkable, celebration on January 6. Called Epiphany, meaning "revelation," the holiday of the three Magi marks the 12th day after Christmas on the liturgical calendar. In many ways Epiphany is the end of the holiday season and the beginning of the cold, dark days of true winter.

As an English teacher in a public school, I often talk about epiphany as a literary term, the moment in a story when a character sees an elemental truth, often painfully, usually unexpectedly, and is forced to reexamine all he knew in light of what has been revealed. The holiday season is full of famous epiphanies—George Bailey in *It's a Wonderful Life* finally realizes that his personal sacrifices have benefited the people of Bedford Falls, and he resumes his dreary life as a reluctant banker with greater enthusiasm. Ebenezer Scrooge in *A Christmas Carol* finally realizes that his personal greed has harmed the people of Victorian London, and he redirects his life as a moneylender with greater compassion.

In my own life, epiphanies have been few and their lessons easily forgotten because my ability to stay grateful or transcendentally aware is limited. For example, a medical scare that turns out to be benign lets me surf along a wave of thankfulness for several days, but the ordinary chores of raising a family and earning a living turn health back into an expectation instead of a gift.

I am a slow learner in school, as well, but as I celebrate this Epiphany I keep thinking about a lesson that a student is teaching me about perseverance.

Shortly after school started in August, one of my students confessed that she had never been in a college preparatory class and was having difficulty with the work.

"I ain't never did nothing like this before," she said, and then quickly amended, "I mean, I ain't never did something like this before."

Try harder, I advised. Keep working, I said, but in the cold, dark winter of my heart I was really saying, Figure this out for yourself. Leave me alone with all my papers to grade and lessons to plan and a new computer program to master. I have too much to do to stop and help you.

She did try harder, and she did keep working, and she did ask me to stop and help her. Sometimes she paused for a minute between classes to show me the notes she had taken or to check over the assignment for the next day. Sometimes she stayed after school to write the essays that she had wrestled with in class but could not finish in the regular class time. Sometimes she brought a list of words from the assigned story and asked me if the definitions she had looked up were correct. Her spirit made me ashamed of my earlier half-hearted encouragement.

When the class began reading *The Scarlet Letter* by Nathaniel Hawthorne, I heard her tell a classmate that she had cut back on her hours at her after-school job so that she could divide the pages by the number of days until the test. Her testimony was responsible for more students actually finishing the novel than any threat or deadline from me.

"This book is really good—once you get past the first thirteen chapters," she told the entire class. "After awhile you forget that it is so hard to understand, and then it starts to mean something."

George Bailey may have had his guardian angel, and Ebenezer Scrooge may have had his ghostly mentors, and even Mary and Joseph may have had the original three wise men, but I have heard the epiphany of a 16-year- old discovering the pride of surmounting a challenge, and it serves as this lesson for me: If we persevere through the difficult parts, after awhile we forget that life itself is so hard to understand, and then it starts to mean something.

And that is an epiphany that will illuminate and thaw out more than just the cold, dark days of true winter.

DESERTS

July 22, 2000

THE DAY WE ARRIVED AT THE DESERT, a hiker died, a victim of extreme conditions: heat so intense and air so dry that it wicked away all the moisture from our faces and chapped our lips before we were ever sunburned. The canyon cliffs and rattlesnakes were clearer dangers; that the invisible atmosphere could kill was a forceful caution about this unfamiliar landscape.

My family and I flew early in June to Phoenix, where large saguaros stand sentry in stone yards and brown mountains guard the horizon. From there we made a two-week circuit through Arizona and southern Utah to see, as my eleven-year-old son called them, all the holes in the ground. Used to green leaves and humidity as slick and hot as dog slobber, we found the arid southwest otherworldly and strangely compelling; yet the hiker's death kept reminding us that for all its alien beauty, the desert is a fearful place, too.

This trip to the desert was a needed escape from another kind of wasteland that began last July when I sat in a Presbyterian Hospital waiting room while my husband had what turned out to be a cancerous section of his colon removed. That surgery marked the beginning of a journey we reluctantly took into the realm of oncology offices and dreary chemotherapy cubicles, of hours of nausea and diarrhea, moments of wrenching fear, and ultimately, my husband's heart attack at Thanksgiving. By spring he was finally finished with the chemotherapy and had recovered enough strength and optimism in the future to plant a vegetable garden.

That's when we started talking about going to the American Southwest. At that time we weren't thinking of the desert as a metaphor for a difficult year. We just wanted to see the landmarks with our sons. We wanted to be awed by the Grand Canyon, amazed by the Colorado River. We wanted to hike among the spindly rock formations known as hoodoos in Bryce Canyon and walk along the Virgin River at Zion National Park. We wanted to ride horses and mules and swim and raft, stay up late and sleep in later, eat too much and follow our impulses.

But the news of the hiker's death transformed the desert into a symbol, a place demanding a stripped-down existence where getting and spending mean more to carry, where the support of family and friends is crucial, where death is a very real possibility, where the sharp contrast of mountain edge and flaming blue sky reminds us, always, that we are mortal.

While we traveled I thought often about the other desert places in my past—the loss of a relationship, a lingering misunderstanding, times of stress and loneliness that left me as bereft and as hopeless as that hiker must have felt when his strength finally gave out—and I have been relieved when my life moved forward into the comfortable predictability of boring days and quiet evenings. I have been glad when I returned to a more temperate land, to a life concerned with cooking supper and doing laundry, to grading papers and planning lessons, able to ignore the ways that I have created deserts for others—a friendship allowed to lapse, a classroom too chilly at times, a kind word unspoken, a good deed unthanked.

Still, not every desert experience is bleak. Just as the real desert hides treasures of loveliness—chocolate-scented flowers and dusky purple lizards, sherbet-hued rock spires and tiny green hummingbirds—the desert of despair can also offer opportunities for unexpected personal growth and a clearer vista of what is real. What burn away are the silly matters that consume us, and what remain tempered and rock-solid are the relationships and values that sustain us. The patient river licking away the sandstone canyon walls tells us that nothing lasts, not even this land. It is a place to feel small and humble, and grateful, too, for the time to be here. It is a place to celebrate surviving.

The day we left the desert, a young Mexican mother did not survive. When the border patrols found her, the infant in her arms was still alive, her canteen half full with water she had denied herself and saved for her baby. As I read the account in the newspaper left in my plane seat, I wondered about the desperation that had fueled that young mother's brave resolve to wrap her child in her shawl and head across the wavering sand, how she must have comforted the whimpering baby and sighed with relief when he fell asleep, rocked by his mother's steady tread. I pictured the mother's eventual stumble, her rising and falling again, exhausted, her trickling water into the baby's mouth, her cradling him and then curling around him when she could no longer sit up, any safe refuge evaporating in the distance like a mirage.

And I thought, finally, that I was glad to be leaving the desert, and when the plane landed I touched my husband's fingers and stepped out into the welcoming humid air.

CRITICAL VIEWING

November 4, 1999

ACCORDING TO THE SYLLABUS I handed out the first day of school, today I begin teaching a unit on film criticism in my senior Advanced Placement English class. Ready or not, I am taking a two-week hiatus from talking about the more familiar media of literature to attempt to explain the history and craft of cinema to students who see more movies in a month than I do in a year. I feel like an impostor discussing television and its effects with the Sesame Street generation.

Everything I know about film criticism I have learned from reading and from observation, which explains in great part why I am so uncomfortable and graceless as I try to teach it.

Literary terms such as symbol and metaphor, characterization and iambic pentameter are comfortable pals; cinematic terms such as best boy and key grip, cinematography and establishing shots are mere acquaintances with whom I haven't spent much intimate time.

Despite my unease, for the past few years I have scheduled an examination of media arts in my AP English class because, like it or not, movies are the literature of modern young people, and movies will continue to be the literature of the 21st century. While I am committed to helping my students understand and appreciate traditional literature, I would be remiss indeed if I ignored the indisputable fact that information increasingly will be gathered through film and TV.

The sad reality is that already fewer and fewer 17-year-olds are coming to my classes genuinely literate. They do not read in their spare time and consequently are not proficient readers. I have become used to students asking me the meaning of ordinary words such as "significance" or "priority" or "ultimate." The vocabulary of adult discourse is a mystery for too many of them, keeping them prisoners in their adolescent ways of thinking and speaking.

If they are not truly literate because they do not read, surprisingly neither are they experts on understanding what they watch on film or television. Listen to typical teenagers discussing the latest movie; rarely do they recognize the cinematic craftsmanship, much less how it affects their emotions and opinions. My students will tell me with intense passion that they like or dislike what they have seen, though they can rarely tell me why. They appreciate the entertainment value of the medium, but that is all.

Learning to look deeper as critical viewers is as important as learning to be critical readers. Critical readers know the various tools available to authors to tell a story; they consider why the artist chooses the tools he does and the effect that choice has on the message being conveyed. Critical readers make reasonable assumptions about an author's meaning when they analyze the tone, the use of irony, the recurring symbols. They are able to read a story on many more levels than just simple comprehension, and their appreciation for the writer's skill adds to their reading enjoyment.

Students experience the same appreciation for film when they know more about how a movie is put together. Recognizing the ability of the camera to direct an audience's gaze is a big step in understanding the power of film—we can look only at what the camera allows us to see; our perceptions are shaped by the lighting, the costuming, the scenery, the sound effects, the music, the camera angles. We are manipulated so skillfully that we do not notice the clever editing which demands that we accept the film's interpretation of reality.

Every year when my students begin to see past the smoke and mirrors of movie making and start to pick apart a film the same way they learn to pick apart a novel, a short story, or a poem, they complain that I have ruined movies for them. What they mean is that they now have some tools for evaluating a movie's artistry, and a teenage slasher movie just isn't as thrilling when the stereotypical characters and the plot are too predictable to be suspenseful.

Critical viewers, like critical readers, are better consumers—less gullible and more resistant to unscrupulous trickery wherever they find it. Imagine what would happen if every American student learned the difference between a manipulative formula movie which rehashes popular culture without anything to teach and the rare thoughtful film which raises the truthful question of what it is to be human. What if American teenagers became alarmed at how their values are being shaped by situation comedies instead of through discussions with their parents and their religious leaders?

They might just turn off the TV and pick up a good book instead.

FREEDOM TO READ

September 23, 2006

MY STUDENTS are reading banned books—or, at least I hope they are, since I assigned them.

This week we began our first one, a tragic story of racial tension, rape, murder, abuse, growth, and redemption. As recently as a few months ago, it was challenged by a parent in Tennessee who contends that its use of racial slurs encourages "racial hatred, racial division, racial separation, and promotes white supremacy."

The book that does all that? *To Kill a Mockingbird.*

No matter that it is widely considered one of the best American novels of the 20th century, or that the admirable characters are the ones who eschew racial hatred at great personal cost, or that the evildoers who embrace racial hatred receive well-deserved justice in the end.

Today is the beginning of the 25th annual Banned Books Week, the American Library Association's celebration of the freedom to read. More than a book a day is challenged or banned in American high schools and public libraries, some, like *To Kill a Mockingbird*, for use of racially charged language, but most because of their depictions of sexuality or the use of profanity.

Regardless of the specific charge leveled against a book, the underlying issue is almost always an offense to the reader's sense of cultural propriety. Although challengers often cite immorality in a particular piece of fiction as a reason for objecting to it, most books which come under fire are, in fact, intensely moral. Traditional values are not questioned at all in even the most troubling adolescent fiction. Good almost always trumps evil; characters endure tough trials, but they learn from them. What are questioned—and often for legitimate reasons—are the traditions and mores of a particular culture.

Great books—the ones which transcend time and place—deal with the broader concerns of human nature. Human nature doesn't change—we all experience the timeless universal emotions of happiness and sorrow, joy and grief, trust and betrayal. People everywhere have always searched for meaning, have needed love and acceptance and community, have wrestled with determining justice and mercy. We still read, thousands of years after it was written, *The Odyssey* because we recognize ourselves in Telemachus as he struggles to establish his credentials as an adult; we know what Penelope is feeling when she cries herself to sleep with longing for her missing husband; we wince when Odysseus faces the dilemma of Scylla or

Charybdis, not because we have ever made such a journey or because we understand all the nuances of ancient Greek life, but because we see ourselves in the story. The cultural references may mystify us, but we understand perfectly the humanity of the characters.

Books that slight this emphasis on the universals of human experience and focus instead on cultural peculiarities soon become dated. Human nature may not change, but cultures inevitably do, vibrating between the comfort of the familiar and the lure of the new.

Our human nature reminds us that we are connected to each other, but our culture serves to narrow our sights into a more manageable tribe or group. It offers us a blueprint for survival and a clan to help insure it—but eventually economic, social, technological, and scientific forces make the rules and ideas of any culture obsolete.

As much as we might desire our traditions to remain the same, change always wins in the end. If it didn't, we would still live in caves, painting the walls and cursing the dark.

People who challenge books worry not only that their culture is slipping beyond their control, but they believe that books can have a pernicious effect on readers. As a writer and as a teacher, I certainly believe in the power of words to hurt or heal, but I also believe in the principle of free speech and the ability of people in a democracy to make informed decisions for themselves.

That's why I support Banned Books Week and will continue putting banned and challenged books on my reading list. Perhaps because their own lives—their own youth culture—is in constant flux, teenagers accept change more gracefully and seem less threatened than their parents by the cultural dissonance in books. For example, when I mentioned to my students that *To Kill a Mockingbird* was often challenged or banned, they were baffled.

"I can see why racial slurs are upsetting," one student said, "but that's how those characters thought and talked. It wouldn't ring true if they didn't. And besides that, the people who complained missed the point of the book completely."

Students who have the freedom to read and who have been encouraged to think critically don't miss the point. They can see through the temporal issues of culture to the eternal concerns of what it means to be human, and they discover their own humanity in the words of people close and far, known and unusual.

HEALTHY SKEPTICS

May 22, 2004

ALMOST 30 YEARS AGO TODAY I graduated from high school. I was third in my class, which isn't particularly impressive in a class of 50. The valedictorian and salutatorian were students more gifted and hardworking than I was, and I don't remember feeling envious of their accomplishments. I was, however, irked that they had the chance to make speeches to the other graduates and the guests while I had to sit mutely in the audience.

The 2004 graduates will probably hear some of the same messages that I heard—to go forth with confidence, to persevere in the face of adversity, to do their best in all things— good messages, certainly, but not the one I would deliver if I had the chance to stand before them and their parents. Instead, my graduation speech would be a call to embrace the character trait essential for becoming a thinking adult. I would tell every graduate to become a healthy skeptic.

A healthy skeptic is someone who rejects easy certainty and intellectual laziness, who actively questions what he sees and hears and doesn't let anyone usurp his mind. All of us are skeptical about people we distrust—we question the accuracy of their data and their motives for sharing it. A healthy skeptic also examines what he learns from his friends and from others who seem to reflect his world view. Even more difficult, the healthy skeptic questions himself, not just what he knows and how he knows, but why he believes what he believes.

Imagine a world of healthy skeptics. We would continue to look at our enemies with a jaundiced eye, surely, but we would be cautious about simplifying their actions into sound bites such as "they hate us because they hate freedom."

When I heard President Bush say this recently about the Iraqi insurgents, my heart sank. What exactly does that mean, that someone hates an abstraction such as freedom? Could some of the Iraqis attacking our troops be motivated by religious fanaticism? Could some of them be fighting because the presence of foreign troops is an offense to their sense of sovereignty? Are some of the insurgents criminals fomenting chaos so that they can profit economically, or could other fighters be interested in carving out a fiefdom of loyalists who will support them in the future after the coalition forces leave them to face each other? Wouldn't we be better off rejecting an easy certainty—"they hate freedom"—and adapting our strategies to deal with a more complex situation?

In a world of skeptics, politics wouldn't trump science. The FDA wouldn't bow to pressure to ignore the recommendations of their scientific panels. The environmentalists who worry about global warming wouldn't be scoffed at by lawmakers who accept campaign contributions from polluters. Treasury Department whistle blowers and terrorist experts wouldn't be squelched or fired. Plagiarized documents touting weapons of mass destruction would undergo genuine scrutiny instead of being used to bolster a particular agenda.

Dissent would be valued as an essential part of sorting out the truth. Discussions would be more raucous debate and less rubber stamping. Censorship would cease to be a concern because people who examine many points of view before drawing conclusions neither want nor need to be protected from information. If we made up our own minds after looking long and hard and skeptically, talk radio would be defunct and political pundits would be out of work.

A world of healthy skeptics would be a world where the charismatic David Koreshes and Osama Bin Ladens would have little power or influence. Fraud would be harder to perpetrate on people who refused to be gullible. Liars would be found out sooner. Lovers might hesitate longer before getting married. Teachers would stop trying to indoctrinate students. Students would hold themselves more accountable.

Most importantly, we would never have a moment when, asked if we could think of any mistakes we might have made, we would draw a blank.

On the last test that I gave my seniors, I realized that

they have become healthy skeptics without hearing any graduation speech from me. In one question I asked them to reflect on their growth this year. What have they learned? How have they changed? What are they taking with them as they leave the nine-month gestation of their senior year?

"I learned to read and write more critically," one student wrote, "but mostly I learned how to think."

Several students wrote that they had learned to listen with an open mind.

"I learned to listen more and talk less."

"I learned that everyone is ignorant, but mostly I've learned that I am, too."

"I've always wondered about that saying that the more you learn, the less you know. Now I understand what that means."

"I know why you have 'the unexamined life is not worth living' on your bulletin board. It's what you really wanted us to learn."

It is indeed.

EPILOGUE

SOCRATES EATS SCHOOL LUNCH

The following remarks were delivered to the Bradley Institute for Christian Culture at Belmont Abbey College on April 12, 2007.

Thank you. I'm honored to be here.

I came to Dr. Preston's attention because of my work with the *Charlotte Observer*. Every other Saturday my column appears on the Viewpoint page, and I usually write about education or other issues which I hope will interest people who care about children. I am very fortunate to have the opportunity to publish my opinions in the newspaper. Most teachers labor anonymously in their classrooms, struggling with many of the same issues that I face, but I get to whine about my tribulations in the *Observer*.

A newspaper is an odd creature. There's a division of labor which journalists observe but which probably goes unnoticed by the reading public most of the time. The majority of a newspaper's resources are devoted to gathering the news, reporting the facts, being as objective as possible when presenting information. And then there is the very much smaller editorial department which comments on the news. In a sense every newspaper recognizes a sort of a Berlin wall between the two separate functions of reporting the news and making commentary about it. The need for reporters is obvious—they are our eyes and ears in government offices, in the community, in the world, extending our vision and our hearing in ways we cannot do alone.

But why does a paper have an editorial department? Who cares what a group of newspaper writers thinks about things? Why not just report the news and leave the interpretation up to the reader?

Just as we can't be everywhere to see and hear what the reporters find, we can't stay on top of all the news all the time and make informed decisions about such a constantly changing landscape. That's where the editorial staff comes in. The news is what they know. I like to think of them as village elders who sit back and listen and watch as the community churns around them with activity. Their view is both broad and deep, and when someone comes to them for advice, they are able to draw on their rich experiences and observations to give it.

Now, depending on your own opinion about a topic, you may think that the editorial writer is more of a village idiot than a village elder, but at least you went through the process of examining your own ideas to make that judgment.

Encouraging that sort of examination is what I do in my newspaper columns as well as what I do in my high school classroom. In fact, on my wall in my room at school I have a huge quotation from Socrates about this subject. "The unexamined life is not worth living," it says. More about Socrates in a moment.

As I said, I am very lucky to have an opportunity to write for the *Charlotte Observer*, something I have been doing since 1999. As many of you probably know, each year the *Observer* has a contest to decide eight new community members to write monthly columns.

Jane McAlister Pope, the deputy editor of the Viewpoint page and the person in charge of the community columnists, spends months reading hundreds of submissions from writers who want to add their ideas to the public discourse through the newspaper.

I didn't know this the year I was chosen. I still remember my first visit to the *Observer* to have my photograph taken and to meet Jane in person. Jane was very pleasant and welcoming, and after a few minutes I finally got up my nerve to ask the question that had been haunting me ever since she called to tell me that I had been selected: "Did anyone else apply?"

I've never gotten up the nerve to ask Jane why I was selected, but I think my introductory letter may have helped. Recently I pulled it back out and looked at it, and it still seems relevant to me today. In the letter I said that I was a lion tamer, a job few people want or really understand. I went on to describe the danger of dealing with hungry, cranky lions, their inherent beauty, the joy of watching them learn, the delight in putting them through their paces. Only then did I say that I was really a high school teacher. Substitute the word "teenager" for "lion" and the letter reads the same, actually.

In some ways all teachers are lion tamers, and we could have an interesting conversation parsing out that metaphor. But I promised that I would talk about Socrates and not Barnum and Bailey.

To explain why this speech is called "Socrates Eats School Lunch," I have to first give you a mental image of my classroom and what I do there. First, picture a large room with a plush gray carpet on the floor. Three of the walls are painted a warm ivory and are decorated with tasteful art reproductions. The fourth wall is a bank of floor to ceiling windows which overlook a neatly kept courtyard where orange and maroon annuals are starting to bloom. Fifteen roomy desks are lined neatly in rows. The room is lit by adjustable incandescent lamps. A cabinet stores a plethora of the newest equipment available to teachers—a large image projector, a remote to work the smart board, a switch to lower and raise a thirteen-foot movie screen. On top of the teacher's desk is a computer running the most up-to-date software. A bookshelf near the door has class sets of books and a wide selection of young adult novels to tempt reluctant readers.

Got that picture? That's not my classroom. That's not any public school classroom that I've ever seen. If while I'm talking you start to imagine that room, don't.

My classroom has no windows. It is lit by fluorescent lights that make a typical fish camp seem dim by comparison. Some of the ceiling tiles are stained brown from leaks in the flat roof. The walls have no tasteful art but are covered with cartoons, *Star Trek* pictures, and demotivational posters. You know what demotivational posters are, don't you? They are wonderful parodies of corporate motivational posters which usually say hearty, inspirational things like "Teamwork builds success" or "It always seems darkest before the morning." My posters say things like "It is always darkest right before it goes pitch black." Some semesters I have thirty-two desks jammed in rows. I do have a computer but I don't think Microsoft still makes software it can run. I have one bookshelf but the books in it are somewhat tattered. One thing wasn't untrue in the first picture I gave you. The carpet *is* gray, at least now.

Keep that image in your mind and add to it about twenty 17 and 18-year-old teenagers. I teach all ability levels of students, but I'm going to show you my Advanced Placement English class, students right at the developmental cusp of learning to think in exciting abstractions. They are bright but rarely like to read—and few read for pleasure these days now that they have so many other possible distractions in their lives. Even the most literate haven't yet recognized what you and I know about literature, that it is one of the best ways to learn who we are. When writers put their thoughts and feelings into words they give voice to all of us. We see ourselves in the narratives of others; we are comforted by our similarities and inspired by our differences. Literature reminds us that we are not alone, that even when we believe that we are caught up in a unique vortex of history, the human condition does not really change. Literature allows us to share the wisdom of those who lived before us, and it offers hope that those who follow us will keep our own expressions alive and meaningful.

For years I have taught Advanced Placement English second block, which for many students is right before lunch. I've had a great deal of freedom in developing the curriculum since AP English is an elective course instead of required for graduation. Students who opt to take it agree to rise to the challenge of college level work and to prove their mastery of the material in May when they take a rigorous exam administered by the College Board, those same people who created the misery known as the SAT.

Bright as they are, these Advanced Placement English students are only now beginning to get a glimmer of the horizon beyond their own concerns. To help them with their vision I often invite Socrates to join the class, and when he does, things get electric.

Socrates, as you recall, was an ancient philosopher who lived in Greece during Athens' freefall from greatness during the Peloponnesian Wars. That quotation on my board—"The unexamined life is not worth living"—comes from one of the pieces of literature my students study, Plato's account of the trial of Socrates. In it Socrates questions his accusers and forces them to acknowledge the inconsistencies in their own thinking. It isn't a trait that endeared him to the Athenians who looked foolish in public.

Socrates—or more precisely, his spirit of playful inquiry—comes to my classroom most often when students and I begin a new unit of study. The literature is divided into the kinds of topics that interested Socrates—truth and justice, for example. Before we read any of the literature dealing with a particular topic, I give the students a list of statements to check as true or false. For example, on our unit on truth, I have a statement that says, "This carpet is gray." Picture my classroom. Easy question, right? The students all say it is a true statement.

"Why did you say the carpet is gray?" I ask a student.

"Because it is," she says. "It looks gray."

"Really? What about now, when I turn the lights off? Isn't the carpet black? It looks black to me. What happened to the gray carpet?"

"It's still gray," the student says, a little concerned that I might be insane. "If you turn the light on you will see that it is really gray."

"But the light isn't on. The carpet looks black. What if you had never seen the carpet with the light on? Wouldn't you say then that its color is black?"

Usually by now the student is getting a bit flustered.

"But I know it is gray," she might insist.

"But how do you know it? Didn't you say that you know it is gray because it looks gray? Aren't you judging the color of the carpet from your own observations?"

"Sure," the student might answer.

"So if you had never seen the carpet in the light, you would never have observed it being gray. You would have only observed it when it appeared black. Wouldn't you say then that the carpet was black?"

At this point we usually have to stop and discuss the nature of light and sight and how they are related to color perception. I get to show off a bit of easy science that the kids have either never learned or never connected to the real world, and they think I'm a genius, at least for a few minutes.

The point of the Socratic discussion—that role of Devil's advocate, always asking more questions and never offering an answer—is not to show off, though. It is to force students to dig beyond their own beliefs, and in the process, to refine their thinking skills. I know the lesson is successful when students throw up their hands and say, "I don't know what I think anymore! This is making my head hurt!" They leave the classroom still in animated discussion, and they take Socrates right on into the lunchroom with them. I can't tell you how many times my students have told me that they continued debating on their own over lunch, garnering weird looks from their neighbors.

Teaching with Socrates isn't easy. The teacher has to be able to outmaneuver her students, thinking quickly on her feet to find and point out the holes in their logic. And a Socratic teacher can't have a dog in the fight, so to speak. By that I mean that she has to be willing to accept any well-argued position a student might take and not be wedded to a particular conclusion. That's why literature lends itself so well to Socratic teaching.

Teaching literature Socratically doesn't mean that we are seeking what Socrates called the essential nature of truth. Instead, we value literature not for some absolute meaning it may have but because it is relevant to our lives.

The critical thinking necessary to make such judgments about literature is also the reason the liberal arts in general lend themselves to Socratic teaching, both in high school and in college.

One of the oldest universities in the country is Yale University, and the preface to the Yale College undergraduate course descriptions recognizes the connection between critical thinking and the liberal arts:

> Yale College offers a liberal arts education, one that aims to train a broadly based, highly disciplined intellect without specifying in advance how that intellect will be used. Such an approach regards college as a phase of exploration, a place for the exercise of curiosity and the discovery of new interests and abilities, rather than the development of interests fully determined in advance. Its goal is to instill in students the development of skills that they can bring to bear in whatever work they eventually choose....Acquiring facts is important, but learning how to think in a variety of ways takes precedence.

Last May Hannah Wallace, one of my graduating AP students, was asked to speak at her church about her reflections on high school. She paid tribute to Socrates and the importance of learning to think this way:

> One of the best decisions I've made in the last year was to take AP English...Like most sen-

iors, I wanted an easy year, but I also really wanted to take this class...Everyone heard the rumors that AP English was long and hard, so that tempted me not to take it...But I had heard that the material was interesting and the books were thought-provoking, so I took my chances and signed up for the class. I didn't get that easy year like I had hoped for....What no one had told me was that this class could be life changing.

I believe Mrs. McSpadden's unspoken challenge was this: Ask yourself the hard questions. She never told us how she felt or her opinions on any topic, but pushed us everyday to ask the really hard questions about life and to think outside the box. We discussed issues like Truth vs. Appearance, Greatness, Love and Hate, Identity, Fate vs. Free Will, and Justice. With each new topic we studied, new questions arose. Questions about what is right and what is wrong; is there a capital T Truth, meaning is there a definite answer that holds true everywhere and in any situation; what makes us who we are; and why do people act the way they do? Before this year, I had never really thought about these questions. I had always believed that I knew what was right or wrong and that I knew who I was, but I had never dug deep enough to find out the whole truth....Instead of remaining passive in my faith, I have asked myself the really hard questions. I believe I have passed

Mrs. McSpadden's challenge. Just like my questions, her challenge was tough. Never once did she say that we had to answer all of the questions, simply research the questions and cherish the journey.

About the same time last May that Hannah was giving her speech, I received an e-mail from Jonathan O'Conner, another former student who showed me that the enjoyment of the journey is what keeps us lifelong learners. He wrote, "Some of the life questions that you posed to us through literature discussions, e.g. 'is man inherently good, evil, or neither?' continue to intrigue me. Now at age 30, however, I am not as curious about your personal answers to those questions. Isn't that timely?"

I'm worried that students like these will not have the opportunities to engage in the give-and-take of Socratic discussions in literature classes in the future. Although most of us here love literature and find it meaningful in our own lives, not everyone does, and unfortunately, some of the skeptics about literature and the other humanities are becoming increasingly vocal. Emory University President James Wagner addressed this growing criticism in a column in the *Atlanta Journal-Constitution* in December 2004. He said that a young professional woman had asked him why anyone should choose a liberal arts education today since it has no practical value and doesn't lead to a career after graduation.

The arts and humanities do not simply entertain us through story, image, music and dance.

They open us up to the mind, heart, and soul of each other. Higher education should make it possible for men and women to lead better lives. But a better life includes not only—and maybe not even especially—greater employability and material comfort. A better life is one freed from ignorance and freed into the life of the mind, to do the work of the world. The true purpose of higher education is to lead us out of our self-centered universe to a place where we can perceive the world from other perspectives and bring understanding and moral imagination to bear on our communities. Higher education should empower us to make a positive impact on society. Higher education is as much about gaining insight as it is about gaining information; as much about seeking wisdom as it is about seeking knowledge.

Emory and Yale and liberal arts institutions such as Belmont Abbey College excel at using art, literature, and history as tools to help students seek wisdom. High schools, however, are being pushed to abandon their emphasis on the liberal arts. Groups such as the New Commission on the Skills of the American Workforce are critical of a high school liberal arts education and are advocating an emphasis on job training instead. In December they released a book length document called *Tough Choices or Tough Times* which was funded by donors such as the Gates Foundation and Hewlett Packard. The Commission recommends ending high school for most students after tenth grade. Only those students who want more preparation before going on to college would stay for a junior and senior year. Everyone else would leave to find employment or go to technical school. Despite increasing evidence that human beings operate with immature brains until our mid 20's, initiatives such as this one would give students fewer opportunities to engage in the kind of Socratic lessons that my seniors talk about over school lunch.

Contrast that to the Yale undergraduate catalog, that requires all students to take courses in what it calls "foundational skills—writing, quantitative reasoning, and foreign language." The catalog goes on to justify those courses by saying, "These skills hold the key to many things students will want to know and do in later study and later life. People who fail to develop them at an early stage are limiting their futures without knowing what opportunities they are eliminating."

In closing, I'd like to give an anecdote about why we need Socrates to keep teaching in our schools and to keep eating school lunch. More than ever we need to resist the idea that acquiring facts is the same thing as getting an education. Our students already believe this, which is why they complain that I make their heads hurt when I force them to reexamine their presuppositions. They want things to be neat and tidy, not open-ended and unanswered. Billy Collins addresses this eloquently in his poem called *Introduction to Poetry*:

> *I ask them to take a poem*
> *and hold it up to the light*
> *like a color slide*

or press an ear against its hive.

I say drop a mouse into a poem
and watch him probe his way out,

or walk inside the poem's room
and feel the walls for a light switch.

I want them to waterski
across the surface of a poem
waving at the author's name on the shore.

But all they want to do
is tie the poem to a chair with rope
and torture a confession out of it.

They begin beating it with a hose
to find out what it really means.

When I gave a test at the end of our unit on Truth to this year's AP students, I included this poem as a cold read, which is English teacher code for a piece of literature that the students have not discussed or possibly even seen before. I can measure my students' growth in analyzing literature by their responses to cold reads because they are really and truly on their own in determining from the literature itself a reasonable explication. At the beginning of the year they are lucky simply to understand basic plot and main ideas. As they become accustomed to treasure diving for the entire range of literary devices, they become sensitized to symbol, parallel structure, irony, metaphor, and so forth. In this particular poem I wanted them to speculate on why Collins says a poem is like a color slide—could this refer to a poem's facility with imagery, perhaps? And when Collins says a poem is a hive, could he be talking about the importance of sound in poetry? Or the mouse in the maze—is he suggesting that part of the fun of a poem is working your way to a reasonable conclusion? And so on.

Because it was our first big unit test, most of the students gave rather sketchy answers, but one student distinguished herself immediately. She pointed out the irony of my asking the class to beat the meaning out of a poem about beating the meaning out of a poem. She argued that the last two stanzas of the poem are clearly a lament about an education system that requires students to do just that. Billy Collins, she said, would have been appalled with my test.

I gave her an A.

BOOKS FOR THE EXAMINED LIFE

HERE ARE THE BOOKS AND PLAYS my seniors read and study through the year. Each one provokes the kind of examined life that I keep striving for—and keep pushing my students and readers to find with me.

THE ODYSSEY BEGINS

Homer, *The Odyssey*. Odysseus may be the best hero ever—smarter than he is strong; aided by divine intervention but hurt by it, too; and above all, human, with all the nobility and frailties that implies.

Joseph Campbell, *The Hero With a Thousand Faces*. Campbell compares heroes through the ages and explains the hero cycle.

Film, Bill Moyers, "The Hero's Adventure" from *Joseph Campbell and the Power of Myth* with Bill Moyers, (Doubleday).

Film, George Lucas, *Star Wars Episode Four: A New Hope* (Lucasfilm). Lucas proves that archetypal heroes resonate with modern audiences.

Athol Fugard, *Master Harold...and the boys.* Fugard's multi-layered play about racism, relationships, and the many ways we fail our children.

Video production of the play (Karl-Lorimar, 1986). Starring Matthew Broderick, Zakes Mokae, and John Kani as the title characters.

TRUTH AND APPEARANCE
Miguel de Cervantes, *Don Quixote.* Playing against type works, as this anti-hero epic shows.

JUSTICE
Job. Beautiful Old Testament poetry which raises troubling questions.

Harper Lee, *To Kill a Mockingbird.* Still frequently challenged, Lee's book weaves several threads of plot together for an unexpected finish.

Film version of *To Kill a Mockingbird* (Universal Studios).

GREATNESS
Film, Nova, *The Pleasure of Finding Things Out* (1987). A documentary about physicist Richard Feynman.

Richard Feynman, *Surely You're Joking, Mr. Feynman* (excerpts). As told to Ralph Leighton, Feynman's inimitable commentaries about life and science.

Film, *Amadeus,* based on the play by Peter Shaffer (Thorn EMI 1984). A Mozart a teen can love.

William Shakespeare, *King Lear.* Perhaps Shakespeare's best play—certainly one of his most heartbreaking.

Film, Akira Kurosawa's *Ran* (CBS/Fox video 1986). King Lear set in 16th century Japan.

FATE AND FREE WILL

Sophocles' *Oedipus Rex.* Tragic and ironic from first to last.

Gabriel Garcia Marquez, *One Hundred Years of Solitude.* My vote for best Latin American novel of the 20th century. Anything can happen and often does in this novel of magic realism.

Film, *Sophie's Choice*, based on the novel by William Styron (Live 1982). When I saw it originally in the theaters, the audience sobbed in unison—loudly. Even teenagers understand the gravity of Sophie's dilemma.

Ian McEwan, *Atonement.* A careless reader might miss the wrenching surprise at the end of the novel. A careful reader is rewarded with immersion into a richly detailed world.

LOVE AND HATE

Film, *Much Ado About Nothing* (Columbia TriStar 1993). A lightly edited version by Kenneth Branagh, starring Branagh and Emma Thompson.

William Shakespeare, *Much Ado About Nothing.* Shakespeare's sparring couples are never more engaging than his Beatrice and Benedick.

John Irving, *A Prayer for Owen Meany.* Often voted the favorite by my students, Irving cleverly alludes to *The Scarlet Letter* and the Bible. Intense, sad, and a hilarious exploration of faith.

William Shakespeare, *Twelfth Night*. As in most of Shakespeare's plays, his women characters are by far the smartest and most honorable. Viola shines as the cross-dressing Cesario.

Film, BBC video production of *Twelfth Night* starring Felicity Kendall (1986).

William Wycherly, *The Country Wife*. An excellent example of what censorship can do—Wycherly's play, like most Restoration comedies, is raunchy and provocative, a deliberate nose-thumbing reaction against the deposed Puritan rule in England.

Oliver Goldsmith, *She Stoops to Conquer*. A comedy about class and manners.

GOOD AND EVIL

John Fowles, *The French Lieutenant's Woman*. Sarah Woodruff is a confounding heroine, and each year my students debate her motives hotly. Fowles' experimental style and intentional imitation of Victorian literature is educational, too.

Flm, *The French Lieutenant's Woman*, starring Meryl Streep (CBS/Fox video 1984).

IDENTITY

Film, Steven Spielberg, *Schindler's List* (Universal Pictures 1997). Was Oskar Schindler a war profiteer or a hero? Spielberg shows both sides of Schindler's character.

Film documentary about Schindler (Thames Video). Many of the *Schindlerjuden* discuss their memories of Plaszow.

Film, *Il Postino* (Miramax 1997). Massimo Troisi's last movie about the son of a poor fisherman who unexpectedly becomes friends with Chilean poet Pablo Neruda.

Ralph Ellison, *Invisible Man.* My vote for the Great American Novel of the 20th Century. An unnamed protagonist is expelled from college, travels North, and becomes involved in The Brotherhood, an obvious parallel to the Communist Party. Ellison links the plot to jazz, African-American folklore, racism, class, sexuality, power.

THE ANTI-HERO'S IDENTITY

Kazuo Ishiguro's *The Remains of the Day.* Stevens, a mild-mannered butler, proves to be an unreliable narrator as he gradually reveals shameful moments from his past.

Film, *The Remains of the Day* (TriStar 1993). A Merchant Ivory production starring Emma Thompson and Anthony Hopkins.

George Orwell, *1984.* So many references from this distopian novel have become iconic that everyone should read it at least once.

THE JOURNEY COMES FULL CIRCLE

Arthur C. Clarke, *2001: A Space Odyssey.* Witty and compelling without being complicated, Clarke's novel explores the nature of evolution and what it means to be human.

Stanley Kubrick's film *2001: A Space Odyssey* (1969). A masterpiece under-appreciated by the *Star Wars* generation, but worthy of review, even if only for HAL's conversation with the doomed astronauts.